MAGIC
PAST LIVES

MAGIC PAST LIVES

Discover the Healing Powers of Positive Past Life Memories

ATASHA FYFE

HAY HOUSE

Carlsbad, California • New York City • London • Sydney
Johannesburg • Vancouver • Hong Kong • New Delhi

First published and distributed in the United Kingdom by:
Hay House UK Ltd, Astley House, 33 Notting Hill Gate, London W11 3JQ
Tel: +44 (0)20 3675 2450; Fax: +44 (0)20 3675 2451
www.hayhouse.co.uk

Published and distributed in the United States of America by:
Hay House Inc., PO Box 5100, Carlsbad, CA 92018-5100
Tel: (1) 760 431 7695 or (800) 654 5126
Fax: (1) 760 431 6948 or (800) 650 5115
www.hayhouse.com

Published and distributed in Australia by:
Hay House Australia Ltd, 18/36 Ralph St, Alexandria NSW 2015
Tel: (61) 2 9669 4299; Fax: (61) 2 9669 4144
www.hayhouse.com.au

Published and distributed in the Republic of South Africa by:
Hay House SA (Pty) Ltd, PO Box 990, Witkoppen 2068
Tel/Fax: (27) 11 467 8904
www.hayhouse.co.za

Published and distributed in India by:
Hay House Publishers India, Muskaan Complex, Plot No. 3, B-2,
Vasant Kunj, New Delhi 110 070
Tel: (91) 11 4176 1620; Fax: (91) 11 4176 1630
www.hayhouse.co.in

Distributed in Canada by:
Raincoast, 9050 Shaughnessy St, Vancouver BC V6P 6E5
Tel: (1) 604 323 7100; Fax: (1) 604 323 2600

Text © Atasha Fyfe, 2013

The moral rights of the author have been asserted.

The information given in this book should not be treated as a substitute for professional
medical advice; always consult a medical practitioner. Any use of information in this book
is at the reader's discretion and risk. Neither the author nor the publisher can be held
responsible for any loss, claim or damage arising out of the use, or misuse, of the suggestions
made, the failure to take medical advice or for any material on third party websites.

A catalogue record for this book is available from the British Library.

ISBN: 978-1-84850-951-1

'Who looks outside, dreams.
Who looks inside, awakes.'

Carl Jung

CONTENTS

LIST OF EXERCISES
AND VISUALIZATIONS

INTRODUCTION

One summer morning a quietly spoken young man came for a past-life regression. I'll call him Garth to protect his privacy – everyone in this book has a pseudonym for the same reason. He felt trapped in a life of boring low-paid work and wondered if there was a past-life cause for this.

In the deep relaxation of a regression, a memory soon came up for him. He went back to a time when he was a young Buddhist monk in the Far East. Coming from a peasant family, he felt inferior to the other monks and was grateful for the chance to live and study at the beautiful monastery.

One night the monastery caught fire. The dazed young monk stared at the flames while his panicky elders scurried up and down with little bowls of water.

Then something within him suddenly took charge. Although he knew it looked like running away, he raced to the nearby village, falling over rocks and scrambling on again until he reached the houses.

Once there, he hammered on door after door, yelling for help and waking up the whole village. Led by their disaster team with its special training and equipment, they all rushed out to fight the fire. The monastery was saved.

Afterwards the monks treated him like a hero. The abbot presented him with a beautiful carving of the Buddha, which he treasured for the rest of his life. Garth said he had a similar carving now that had always been strangely important to him.

A few months later, he phoned me with some good news: he'd finally landed a better job. He said he was sure the memory of saving the monastery had given him the confidence to start climbing the ladder of success.

That regression was a turning-point for me as well. It got me thinking about the importance of positive past-life memories. In my hypnotherapy practice, positive memories had naturally come up at times and I'd thought they were pleasant enough but didn't get down to the 'real' issues. Now I began to wonder if they might have some major therapeutic benefits of their own.

Like most healing modalities, regression therapy tends to focus on people's problems. But is this really the only way?

When past-life therapy began over 50 years ago, it was a tiny seedling that had to struggle against the heavy winds of conventional resistance. Through the courage of the pioneers, it has now grown into one of the most successful ways to resolve personal issues.

It works because current problems are so often rooted in negative past-life experiences. While the conscious mind doesn't remember them, their effect remains within the psyche like an unhealed wound. As long as they stay unconscious, these old traumas have the power to control our behaviour and thus our lives. When we become aware of them, they lose that power over us.

'Other therapies address the symptoms and leave the cause untouched. Past-life therapy attacks the root cause,' said clinical psychologist Dr Edith Fiore.

This is a wonderful discovery that has helped countless numbers of people. But what if our past lives have even more to offer us?

I began to wonder why we had so many lives if all they ever gave us was wounds to be healed. Maybe there was a positive side to our reincarnational history. Some of our former selves might turn out to be our greatest allies – a source of the confidence, self-worth and strengths that we need most in our lives now.

So I decided to collect and research people's positive past-life memories. After all, focusing only on negative experiences is like trying to be healthy with nothing but medicine. We also need good food.

As this project progressed, I noticed that the most satisfying and significant past lives weren't about worldly success for its own sake. They weren't bland walks in the park either – they had their dramas and challenges, which gave them meaning and structure.

The lives people felt best about were those that had followed an inner purpose. They might have brought major turning-points, discoveries and revelations, or significant personal growth. They often held special knowledge about spiritual and esoteric matters.

My research showed that those truly positive past lives were the high points on the soul journey and had much to offer in the present. As well as bringing personal benefits, they could put us in touch with lost wisdom and forgotten abilities from worlds long past.

Perhaps in the future this valuable information may be pooled for everyone's benefit. Occasional memories, although they may well be valid, can't be said to prove anything. But if a long-term data bank of many regressions were built up and analysed in a systematic way, it could be used to supplement other methods of historical research.

The psychologist Dr Helen Wambach showed that this could be done. In the 1970s she took on the huge project of regressing hundreds of people, roomfuls at a time, to specific periods in history. Afterwards they filled in detailed forms about what they'd got and the results were analysed.

The memories turned out to be uncannily accurate. The descriptions of clothing, coinage, footwear, social structures, architecture, cooking methods, eating utensils and diet were all found to be historically correct.

Around the same time, British journalist Jeffrey Iverson did an in-depth investigation of hypnotherapist Arnall Bloxham's work. He called on experts to check every obscure historical detail that was mentioned in Bloxham's taped regressions. By the end of that project he was satisfied that the past-life memories were valid.

In his book about this, *More Lives Than One?*, he said, 'If society ever accepted the notion that people under hypnosis could be regressed to have reliable knowledge of other times, the study of history would be revolutionised.'

That day may be coming. Academies of past-life research could be set up, giving everyone's personal memories the chance to make a significant contribution.

How we get those memories may also evolve. At present, people who want to access a former life usually go to a regressionist. But in time we may all find we can get that information easily enough by ourselves.

This is because regression is simply a matter of relaxation. Relaxation takes us into a natural state of altered consciousness. On a graph, the busy everyday 'beta' brainwaves look like choppy water, with lots of shallow spikes. The more relaxed alpha brainwave shows up on the chart like a peaceful rolling ocean. The next stage down is called theta, which is going into a trance state. After that is delta, which is deep sleep. But the alpha level of deep relaxation while still conscious is all that's needed to access past-life memories.

Our everyday mental state is like driving. It narrows our focus onto the task in hand – the road ahead – so we barely get a glance at the surrounding scenery. More relaxed states of mind are like going for a stroll. They give us the chance to enjoy the panoramic vistas of our greater awareness.

To put it another way, it's like looking at life through the different windows of a house. At the ground-floor level of the beta state all we can see is our own garden. As we relax, it's as if we can look through higher windows and see the wider countryside beyond the garden wall.

What we see from that vantage point depends on where we focus our attention. The only limitations come from what we believe is possible.

While in the alpha state it's possible to access not only past lives but also higher guidance. This could be from a guardian angel, a personal guide or our own inner wisdom. I've found this kind of advice helps enormously in understanding past lives and how they can help our lives now.

In the deep alpha state, many people also remember where they went after they died. In my research and experience no one has ever reported any kind of judgement or condemnation there – even when it was expected. All the reports show that the afterlife worlds are first of all places to rest and recover. Later on there may be discussions with friendly guides about the life just passed and what to do next.

While those themes are constant, the places people find themselves in are full of rich variety.

'Some people go over and find pure energy and light. And yet I have many who say they see beautiful lakes, beautiful scenes, gleaming cities,' said Dr Edith Fiore.

The good news is that it's not necessary to wait for the afterlife to experience higher-dimensional reality. When we see life through the upper windows of a relaxed mind, we can discover:

◈ An overview of our soul journey.

◈ Insights about our current life purpose.

◈ Positive, spiritually empowering past-life memories.

◈ Lost ancient knowledge.

◈ Past-life talents and abilities.

◈ A new understanding about others in our life.

◈ Ways to contact spirit guides and guardian angels.

◈ Memories of the afterlife worlds.

When it's time to unearth your past-life connections, memories may begin to come into your dreams, or your meditations or visualizations. Pictures or references to times and places could start popping up, as if asking to be noticed.

If you make a note of these dreams, signs and synchronicities, you'll begin to see a pattern emerge. It's like slowly putting a jigsaw together. Even when it's incomplete, after a while you can get a good idea of the whole picture.

You could ask for more information in your dreams or meditations. If you feel apprehensive, call on your guardian angels and spirit guides for help and protection.

When you gather past-life information like this – little by little, and in your own time – the pieces of your bigger picture will fall into place at just the right moment for you.

Stories can be good past-life memory joggers. One of the accounts in this book may ring a bell for you. A certain era, place or way of life could feel curiously familiar. Perhaps the tale of a questing knight, mysterious lady or herbal healer will whisper hints to you about one of your forgotten selves.

A bit of quiet musing is often enough to start nudging sleepy old memories awake. The guided meditation exercises at the end of each section are designed for that kind of safe and gentle recall. Using the main symbols of each section as a gateway, you can view scenes from your past lives for as long or briefly as you wish.

Bit by bit, you'll be able to piece together the bigger picture of your soul journey and your many positive discoveries and achievements. In this way, your past-life explorations will become an integral part of your ongoing journey of soul exploration.

Along the way, past-life magic will work its spell of transformation: neither you nor the world you live in will ever be the same again.

PART I
SHAMANIC WORLDS

*'The shaman is a self-reliant explorer
of the endless mansions of a magnificent
hidden universe.'*
Michael Harner

INTRODUCTION

Some years ago, a friend told me the story of his nature magic experience. It happened at Chalice Well, in Glastonbury, Somerset.

About 20 of us were sitting in a circle in the upper field. We were singing healing songs. After a while I closed my eyes and just let the sounds wash over me. And I went into a kind of time shift.

It felt as though I'd gone way, way back. I was still sitting in a circle, but the people were different. They were rougher – closer to the earth.

After a moment or two it faded and I was back in the present. I don't know why I had that experience. But it was so real I've never forgotten it.

Since then I've regressed so many people who have gone back to the times of nature magic that I think shamanic consciousness is waking up again. Our past selves from that world seem to be calling to us. Or are we calling to them?

If we are, it's hardly surprising. The modern world has become so materially focused that our culture is losing any sense of the mystery of life. Maybe in reaction, people are harking back to times when they experienced the Earth as a place of magic and wonder.

In many ways, our past selves from those times are also coming to meet us. As they do, they bring new expressions of the old ways back into our world.

The Native American Lakota people have a beautiful prayer, *Mitakuye Oyasin*, meaning 'We are all related.' Respect for the spirit within each living thing is at the core of all shamanic cultures.

After centuries of insensitive exploitation, ecological and conservation awareness is now restoring our ancient regard for nature. Many an organic gardener or animal rescuer may be subliminally drawing on attitudes now stirring in the forests of ancient memory.

Shamanic healing focuses on the spirit realm as the true origin of any physical problem. This principle is now returning, with new awareness of how thoughts and emotions affect our physical wellbeing. Modern therapeutic methods have begun to treat the body holistically – as shamans always have done – rather than as a collection of mechanical parts.

A growing number of people now mark the seasonal turnings of the year at solstice and equinox. These celebrations reaffirm the old cyclical view of time. They reconnect us at deep levels with our ancient faith in the return of the sun and life after death.

It's as if we've come full circle. The intuitions of traditional people, long dismissed as superstition, are being scientifically proved. The old ways are turning out to be both realistic and life-enhancing.

Past lives in shamanic realms create a strong bond with Mother Nature. We emerge from them with a heartfelt appreciation of her abundance, mystery and power. The experience establishes a foundation of security within the psyche which becomes a major source of strength in later incarnations.

Under the great umbrella of that main effect, there are also a multitude of personal aims and benefits. One of my clients found that he'd undertaken a shamanic life because he wanted to heal his relationship with animals. Another recalled patching up a major quarrel between two tribes – and became aware of how she'd been ignoring her talent for diplomacy.

A third remembered a life of climbing high trees to get food and building materials for his community. Working at heights was a theme that ran through many of his subsequent lives. In his current life the 'heights' he was aiming for were more symbolic than literal, but the memory shored up his courage, showing him that he could do it.

When a memory is ready to surface, all kinds of reminders may wake it up. Anthea went to a site of ancient standing stones and was surprised at the strong feelings of excitement and yearning that it brought up in her. When she got home, she decided to investigate her reaction. She focused her mind on that place and drifted into a relaxed meditation.

In the memory that came up she found herself there again, very long ago. A white-robed man put a wreath of oak leaves on her head and gave her a drum. She sensed that this was a Druid ceremony. Although brief, the memory felt significant. It also gave her a message about her present life.

When I saw her again some months later, she told me that out of curiosity about that memory, she'd taken up drumming. She discovered that she enjoyed it and found it easy to learn. Previously rather nervous and highly strung, she had a new air of calm confidence. She was drumming her way back to the inner resilience of an earlier life.

Any physical re-enactment can be a powerful memory prodder. Ancient rituals, chants and dances all have the potential to stir up long-forgotten feelings.

Early on the morning of the day Billie went to a Native American dance workshop, when she opened the curtains she was amazed to see large numbers of crows outside. Dozens of them were pecking around in the road. Many more were perched in long lines along the rooftops, electric cables and street lights. This was so unusual she knew it meant something, but had no idea what. It wasn't long, however, before she found out more:

> Once I got to the workshop I forgot all about the crows. I was so happy to be doing those dances and singing those songs. I don't know why, but it meant a lot to me. Then, part way through, the teacher suddenly told us that for Native Americans, the crow was an important messenger of spirit. He said it was a great honour to be called 'crow woman'. So, after those synchronicities, I'm wondering if I was a Native American in a previous life.

Billie's regression follows in the next chapter. As she and many others have found, past-life gifts sometimes come wrapped in strange and surprising ways.

1

THE MESSAGE OF THE CROWS

New ideas usually have to run a tough gamut of resistance from the old ways. So it feels appropriate that the first account in this book is about a dramatic encounter between two very different mindsets.

Billie's experience with the crows and the Native American dance workshop made her curious about past lives. She came for a regression partly about that, but mainly because she felt that her life was in a rut.

'Nothing is moving. Nothing changes,' she said. 'Things always used to flow. But it's just not happening anymore. So, after that experience at the workshop, I wondered if something from a past life might help.'

Billie took easily to the regression and soon saw herself on horseback riding next to a long and dusty wagon train. This was America in the early days of expansion into the Wild West.

She was a young girl wearing men's clothes, partly because it was more practical and partly because she'd always been a bit of a tomboy. Her family was travelling in one of the wagons, while she and her brother were among those who rode alongside. She said they did this partly to make the wagons lighter and partly to look out for danger.

AF: *What sort of danger?*

B: *Attacks from Red Indians, I suppose.*

AF: *Has that ever happened?*

B: *No. We try to avoid Indian country. But there's still a long way ahead.*

It looks as though the leaders want to stop now and set up camp. It'll be dark soon. There's a little creek here for water. Yep – there goes the call, right down the line to the back: 'Everyone stop.'

(Pause)

It's night-time now. They're all sitting round the campfires. I've gone for a little walk. The sky is full of stars. I love being out here. I wish I could live like this forever.

(After a long silence, Billie started showing signs of distress.)

AF: *What's happening?*

B: *Indians! They suddenly appeared from nowhere – hooping and screaming, letting fly with their arrows, attacking our wagons. There are gunshots, screaming, a lot of noise...*

An arrow came straight into my leg. Then one of them rode fast at me, grabbed me and pulled me onto his horse. He's riding off with me. I'm struggling, trying to get away. But he's strong. He hoiks me back again.

(Pause)

I'm in their settlement now. There are a lot of little tents. I'm off the horse. He's got me tied by the wrists and is leading me along, shouting things.

The people come running to see. They stand staring at me. I suppose he's going to kill me now.

An old man has come... they talk for a bit. Then my kidnapper follows him, pulling me along behind.

They put me down on some sort of bed. I'm in a cave. It looks as if somebody lives here. The old man is talking to my kidnapper over at the entrance.

He goes. The old man comes at me with a rag and a bowl of something. I'm scared. He wets the rag from the bowl and puts it on the arrow wound. I'm trying to push him away. He gets me to drink something.

The wound is starting to feel numb. He keeps the rag on it. He's crooning something... over and over, up and down, over and over. I'm starting to feel woozy... everything is drifting away...

(Deep sigh)

I don't know how long I've been asleep. It's hard to wake up. The old Indian is standing grinning at me. He mimes that I slept after he gave me the drink and then he took the piece of arrow out of my leg. There's a whole wodge of dressing on the wound. He's showing me that I should leave it alone and then it will heal. He gets me to drink something again.

Now I'm just lying there watching him. He's pottering around his cave, singing his funny little song. I'm feeling as though I could lie here forever.

(Sounding drowsy) I hope my family are OK. My brother will probably get up a gang to come and rescue me. Hope they come soon. Before these Indians sacrifice me. Or whatever they do.

Time passed, her wound healed and nobody came to rescue her. The medicine man was treating her kindly, but as soon as she could walk again, she decided to escape and get back to her own people.

> (Whispering) *It's early morning. The old man is snoring in his little bed at the back of the cave. I'm sneaking off.*
>
> (Later)
>
> *I'm at the place where we made camp the night before the attack. It looks as though they left in a big hurry – there are lots of bits and pieces lying around that they'd normally take with them.*
>
> *So they left without me. Maybe they gave me up for dead.*
>
> *My leg is hurting like hell. It's getting dark now. I'm going to have to spend the night here. I hope some wild animal doesn't get me.*

After a frightening night in the wilds, she tried to follow the trail of the wagons. But by then she could hardly walk.

> *I'm lying on the ground. I must have blacked out or something. There are two Red Indians standing over me. They pull me up and put me across a horse. I'm too weak to fight them.*
>
> *This is it. My life really is over now. And I thought I was going to have such a good time, exploring the new world and everything.*
>
> *Now I'm back in the cave with the old man. He's giving me more of that woozy juice. I'm passing out.*

As time went by, her wound healed completely.

> *The old man has been teaching me things. I'm learning their language, which plants to gather for healing, how to turn them into medicine...*

He told me that whenever I was looking for something I should sing its song. He said I'd find it more easily if I did that. He started teaching me all these little chants to sing. I felt a bit dumb doing that at first. But then I started to like it. And it does seem to help. When I sing the little songs, I always find things.

He has also shown me how to tell what the weather will be like and how to read omens and signs. I didn't believe any of that to start with, but then as I went along, I saw it working.

It feels good to look at the day and watch for the signs. It's handy stuff to know. It gives me something to do while I'm waiting.

AF: *What are you waiting for?*

B: *I can't find my people by myself – I'll just get lost – so I'll have to stay here for a while longer. But sooner or later someone's bound to find me and take me back. I've got so much to tell them!*

The old man sees it differently, though. He said he knew someone like me was going to come. When he saw me he knew I was the one he'd been waiting for. That's why he had to look after me and teach me their ways.

AF: *How did he know that?*

B: *Oh, he has dreams and visions and that sort of thing. He says the spirits sent me to them.*

AF: *How do you feel about that?*

B: *That's just his stuff – it doesn't matter to me. The big thing is I'm not scared of them anymore. And I like the things I'm learning here.*

(About a year later)

I don't think anyone is going to come and get me now. They gave me up for dead long ago, so I may as well forget about them. And I'm learning all these interesting new things here. I don't even want to go back anymore.

The old man says I'm good at getting messages from the birds. I see the way they move in the sky as a feeling – like a dance. Then I say what I think it means. He says this is my special gift. He's going to teach me how to use it more.

One day she was allowed to join in one of the tribe's big ceremonies:

The old man has been teaching me their big songs for a while – the songs they all sing together at these gatherings. There are two girls giggling and painting my face and hanging feathers and beads all over me. It's kind of fun.

(Later)

Memories of the gathering are coming now... It was so wonderful. I sang all the songs with them... I joined in their dances round the circle... It felt so good I cried. They laughed and dabbed my face so my paint wouldn't run. It was the best time I've ever had in my life. I'm truly one of them now.

(Long pause)

AF: *Where are you now?*

B: *In the same place. I've been here for years and years. The Indians are my people now. My life is here. I'm happy with it.*

I'm the old medicine man's helper now. I can only be his helper, not his apprentice, first because I'm female and secondly because I'm not of their blood. But I don't mind.

I'm with him and one of the other elders now. It's night. We're sitting on a hilltop looking at the stars.

They're saying we came out here because they have some special things to tell me. They couldn't tell me before because these things aren't for the ears of outsiders. But I'm one of them now, so it's OK.

I'm sitting between the two of them. The medicine man is talking and the other one is drumming softly.

It's a clear night. We're looking at the great Milky Way. He's talking about how big the sky is, pointing out some of the stars, telling me stories about them. He says his people have brothers and sisters who live up there in the stars. Long ago they came here and taught them everything they know.

He says we can still talk to them from here. They're going to show me how to do that.

They start by calling to them with a special song – the star song. Then we must open our hearts and minds. They show me the hand movements that mean we're doing that. Then we must sit quietly for maybe a long time and just wait for a sign.

They've started singing their star song. It's so beautiful. I'm looking at the stars while they do that.

Now I'm floating high up in the sky. I can see the three of us looking very small and far away, sitting on the hill. The starry sky is all around me.

I'm drifting higher and higher... I've gone away from it now...

(Long pause)

I'm back to who I am now, in the twenty-first century, but the medicine man is still with me. We're walking along together. He's telling me things he says I wasn't ready to understand when I was in that life. But he can tell me now.

He says there was a good reason for me to go and live with them. I needed a spiritual shot in the arm. It came as an arrow in my leg.

He says that was a multi-dimensional event because it had many layers of meaning. On the one level, it was simply a brutal attack. He says the man who did it will face his own karma about that.

On a higher level, in my soul I knew I needed something to pierce the heavy armour that I'd built up over lots of lifetimes. It took that arrow to open me up to spirit. But he also says I was really stubborn. I fought it for a long time. When I finally accepted things, it all went well.

He says this memory has come up now partly to remind me and partly because the same pattern is repeating in my life now. Not as dramatically, though – it's just a faint echo of what happened back then.

This is why I've been feeling stuck – it's because I've been unconsciously fighting the new and trying to hold on to the old. That will change now. Remembering this life will free me from that.

The crows came to wake me up and to let me know that I really did become one of his people. That's why the dancing and singing meant so much to me at the workshop.

He says that deep down I've always had a lingering doubt, a feeling that I didn't really make it – wasn't good enough or something. He says the crows came to let me know that I did succeed. The purpose of that life really was fulfilled.

(At that, she became a bit tearful.)

He says that's it for today. He'll see me again. He waves goodbye, then turns and walks away.

2

WHERE THE CLUES HIDE

Sipping a restorative cup of tea after the regression, Billie was delighted to realize that her strange past life had had a higher purpose and had ended so well.

'It was all worth it,' she said. 'Even the arrow wound had a spiritual meaning.'

She began to wonder about signs that had always pointed to that life, even though she hadn't understood them at the time:

I've always had a dimple at the top of my thigh – in exactly the place where that arrow went in. The other thing was, when I was about six I was watching an old cowboy movie and one of the scenes really freaked me out. I can see it so clearly in my mind's eye, even now. It was an arrow thudding into a wooden wall right next to a woman's head. I didn't have the words for it, but my feeling was, How can they turn this into entertainment? Don't they know how terrifying it is? I was even sick afterwards. I threw up.

I said it made complete sense. She'd reacted that way to the movie because it had touched on her memory of the ambush.

Clues about our past lives can pop up in all kinds of unexpected ways. As Billie found, they are even more powerful if they come to us in childhood.

The Magic Memory of Childhood

Studies have shown that it's normal for young children to be in touch with their past-life memories. When they are under the age of eight, their earlier lives flit just below the surface of consciousness like faintly visible fish.

In the very first days of life, those memories may be even clearer than that. A Tibetan medical text from the eleventh century says: 'In the 26th week in the womb, the child's awareness becomes very clear and it can see its former lives.'

The western world is only now catching up with this ancient knowledge. In the 1970s Professor Ian Stevenson, head of psychiatry at the University of Virginia, did extensive research showing just how much young children were in real touch with their previous lives.

He amassed over 2,600 accounts of children whose former-life memories passed his many stringent tests. Out of those he picked 20 to publish in his book *Twenty Cases Suggestive of Reincarnation*.

As a careful academic, Dr Stevenson shied away from calling his findings 'proof'. But he did say that he felt these children's memories were valid and significant, stating that 'Often a child begins fumbling at the age of two, or even less, to communicate his memories of a previous life.'

These fumblings usually take the form of passing remarks about another family, a home elsewhere, or their old work. Snippets like this are all too easy to dismiss or ignore, and the child soon forgets about them.

In her book *Children's Past Lives*, Carol Bowman explained how to catch those slippery statements – and gently ask for more. After much research and experience, she nailed down the following signs that a child is telling the truth about another lifetime:

◈ A matter-of-fact tone of voice.

◈ The details of the story stay the same at every retelling.

◈ When talking about their past self in the first person, they sound more mature.

◈ Their behaviour and other signs back up the statements.

An experience which ticked all those boxes occurred while she was bathing 18-month-old Elisabeth.

'I'm going to take my vows,' the infant suddenly announced. 'I'm not Elisabeth now – I'm Rose. But I'm going to be Sister Teresa Gregory.'

The toddler chattered away about obscure minutiae of daily life in a convent – things that even her mother hadn't known. Upon research, all those details were found to be correct.

Lofric and Wofric

Children may also act out past-life dramas in their games. When I regressed her, Cathy recalled a British tribal life during the time of the Roman occupation.

Cathy and her present-life brother, both men at the time, lived deep in the woods and raided Roman settlements now and then. The man Cathy had been was killed on one of those forays.

After that memory had come up, Cathy suddenly recalled something she hadn't thought about for years:

When I was a child, the house next door had a wonderful plum tree and my brother and I would pinch some of the fruit. We weren't short of food at home. It was just for fun, and the adventure.

We'd call ourselves Lofric and Wofric. We'd get cloths from the kitchen and laundry basket and tie them onto ourselves. I think I can see why we did that now: when we raided the Roman settlements, we used to disguise ourselves with leafy branches, so maybe tying these cloths on ourselves was an echo of that.

Then one day the old man came out and saw us taking his plums. He stared at us and we stared at him. I was so terrified I felt paralysed.

Then he gave a little shrug and a funny smile, and turned around and went back inside. We dashed away as fast as we could. I think those expeditions fizzled out after that.

Cathy wondered if this childhood memory had come up because of a connection to the past life she'd just recalled.

'Maybe we had to play that out to get some sort of closure about it,' she said. 'It was wonderful that the man didn't react badly – yell at us or complain to our parents or whatever. It released me in some way.'

Was that old man the Roman soldier who had killed Cathy all those centuries ago? We will probably never know. But whoever he was, his kindly tolerance gave a sad old story a happy new ending.

How the Body Holds Past-Life Clues

Our bodies hold past-life memories for us in our health, strengths, weaknesses, movements, tics, posture and appearance.

'Body language is like dream language. It gives you indications that the conscious mind is not yet able to give,' said author and therapist Arnold Mindel.

Like Billie's dimple where the arrow went in, a past-life wound sometimes shows up on the body in the form of a birthmark. Dr Stevenson discovered that birthmarks could appear in exactly the same place on the body as a death blow from a previous life. The marks may even look just like an old scar from the fatal knife, bullet or strangling wire.

These synchronicities have long been taken for granted by folk traditions around the world. In Burma, children who remember their past lives are called *winzas*. If a child dies, or is near death, the Burmese put a special ceremonial mark onto that child's body. When a baby later appears bearing that mark, they take it as a sign that the lost child has now come back.

The Tlingits of Alaska welcome babies with birthmarks that look like those of deceased elders. They say it means that person has returned and they give the baby the same name.

British Columbians believe babies born with teeth already growing or dimples in their earlobes are reincarnated ancestors. The teeth are a sign that the baby has an advanced soul; the ear dimples come from lots of past lives with pierced ears.

Birthmarks can have dramatic tales to tell. One of the most famous has to be ex-Soviet President Gorbachev's big red mark on his head. It looks like the bloodstain from a heavy blow. With his strong sense of political mission, I wouldn't be surprised if Gorbachev was murdered in a past life by those who wanted to stop him. His victorious return shows that the spirit can never be killed and that nothing can stop us from following our higher purpose.

Samskaras

Ancient yoga teachings say that we have an inner subtle body which goes from one life to the next. All our experiences on the earthly plane affect this spirit body. It can be weakened and wounded or brightened and refined. The next time we incarnate, the spirit body imprints the new physical body with those effects, which are called *samskaras* in Sanskrit.

Many of these imprints are positive. But in each lifetime, there are usually one or two *samskaras* that will come up for healing. They often present themselves as physical issues. The soul sends important messages to us through our bodies. As we address those problems, we heal so much more than just an old physical wound – we also heal the wound to our spirit.

Holistic therapies which treat the mind, body and spirit as one can help in many ways to heal past-life issues that are held in the body. Even simple bodywork can have a surprising effect.

In the middle of a relaxing massage, a woman I know suddenly realized what her relationship problems were really about. She saw that she'd been with her partner in a former life, but in the opposite roles – she had been the man and he the woman. As a woman in that life he'd been overly clingy and dependent. The problem was that he was unconsciously trying to go back to those ways. Suddenly everything fell into place. She understood exactly what was going wrong – and also how to put it right.

A therapist friend told me that he sometimes found etheric spears, knives and arrows stuck in his clients' subtle bodies. This was because the emotional effects were still there. People might also still be wearing inner ropes, handcuffs or chains from a past life.

Knowing why these objects are there makes it easy to remove them. After that, the inner wounds heal quickly.

Along the way, other problems may get resolved as well. Healing major issues can work like a catapult, shooting the person higher and further along their spiritual path than they would have gone otherwise.

Billie felt that certainly applied to her:

> Perhaps in some way that arrow wound was a kind of vaccination. I now feel that I've gone back to being the kind of person I was when I joined the wagon train. Not the stubborn side – maybe that's what I got vaccinated for! – but the adventurer.
>
> I was always carefree and go-for-it – in this life too, at least initially. But somewhere along the line that got left behind. I can see now how closed off and stick-in-the-mud I'd been getting. Maybe that's why my life got stuck. This memory has brought me back to my real self. I think life is going to be different from now on.

Not all *samskaras* are wounds to be healed. They can also be sources of strength. Linda told me of her strange experience while working as a messenger in London. The job meant walking long distances every day; she couldn't take the tube or bus because she had to drop into so many places in between the stops:

> At first it really tired me out. My feet were so sore at the end of the day that I didn't think I'd last a week in that job. But then I had a strange breakthrough.
>
> One day I found I'd gone into a kind of hypnotic walking. It felt as though I was taking long loping strides. As if I was hardly touching the ground – although I'm sure I looked perfectly normal to everyone else. But I felt like another person – a tall man who was a tribal messenger.

*I had to walk very long distances in that life as well. But
I did it with this special way of walking and that came
back to me while doing that job. It was as if my body
remembered how to do it and just took over.*

*I think I would have dismissed it as fantasy except for one
thing – the walking didn't tire me out anymore. I think
my body solved the problem by calling on a past self who
knew how to handle it.*

The Wisdom of the Body

The body has a wisdom of its own. It holds our past-life
memories until we're ready to deal with them. Its ailments
can be important messages to us. It looks after us in so many
ways that go beyond the simply physical.

In shamanic tradition, the initiate was said to be
torn to pieces and then put together again with magical
powers. Crises, wounds or illnesses that brought a spiritual
breakthrough were signs that the Great Spirit had chosen
you for a higher role.

For most of us, those ways are from such a different
world that we don't expect to go through anything like that.
But shamanic initiations were based on the natural way in
which the spiritual path unfolds for everyone. Even though
our culture doesn't have any special rituals for it, the same
process still takes place in our lives.

Knowing this makes it possible for anyone to transform
life's tests by understanding their higher meaning – a process
which is at the heart of traditional shamanic initiation.

3

PLANT CONSCIOUSNESS

A n ancient mystical relationship with nature weaves like a green vine around our memories of shamanic times. In those days we knew that every living thing had a spirit. Because of that, we respected all forms of life and knew their secret languages. Mother Nature shared her boundless stores of nurturance and healing with us, and we honoured that in our rituals and ceremonies.

In her regression, Kass described a life that was devoted to those ways. She lived in a small community in the woods. She and her two sisters were the respected elders of the little tribe:

We live in huts made of wood... animal hides... stone... mud. Moss is stuffed into all the gaps. They're quite snug and cosy. The back walls of the huts are joined together and made strong. They make a protective wall around us.

My sisters and I live in a special big hut with all our medicines and a place to give healing to people. We work with the inner spirits of plants, trees and animals. Nature shows us how to make good medicine – how to do special magic for healing.

We can see things that are in the forest. The men consult us before they go hunting. When the spirit of the animal is willing, it shows us where to find it.

We can see what's coming. We feel it on the wind. We know when bad weather is on the way. We can see sickness in a person before they know it themselves.

Kass was describing an ancient matriarchal society which worked in harmony with nature rather than trying to control and dominate it. Since leaving those ways behind, western civilization has come to see plants and animals as nothing but physical objects for the service of humankind.

'For centuries, westerners have been spiritual deaf-mutes who have forgotten how to communicate with nature,' said the Peruvian shaman Eduardo Caldero'n Palomino.

In recent decades, however, the tide has been steadily turning. That began with a handful of researchers who had the courage to stand up to the established mores. Lyall Watson's book *Supernature*, *The Secret Life of Plants* by Tomkins and Bird, and Rupert Sheldrake's extensive research and writings have all shown beyond doubt that nature has its own consciousness.

In his book *The Holographic Universe* Michael Talbot said, 'Even a rock is in some way alive, for life and intelligence are present not only in all of matter, but in energy, space and time – the fabric of the entire universe.'

These discoveries have also walked out of the books and into real life. While in Glastonbury in the 1960s, Eileen Caddy experienced a spiritual revelation about her life's purpose. Following their inner guidance, she and her husband Peter went to live near the village of Findhorn in Scotland. There they planted a vegetable garden. To help it along, they began to commune with the spirits of nature. Within a few years, they were famous for the gigantic vegetables they were producing simply by talking to their plants.

The Findhorn Foundation is now one of the largest international eco-centres in Britain, with thousands of residents from all over the world, though they aren't growing giant vegetables anymore. Someone who taught at Findhorn for many years told me that this was because the nature spirits had let them know that it was no longer necessary. The point had been made, and growing to unnaturally huge sizes was a strain on the plants. The Foundation's work now focuses on ecology, alternative medicine and book publishing.

The latest eco-centre to produce plant miracles is Damanhur. From a small beginning at the foot of the Piedmont Alps in Italy, the Damanhur Foundation is now an international force, with branches in Europe, Japan and America.

They've been experimenting with plant communication since 1975 and have now invented a device that can trace electrical changes in a plant. All living things produce fluctuating electrical signals as they react to the world around them. The Damanhur device shows how strongly plants respond when they are spoken to or watered.

The researchers also found a way to translate those responses into music. Once the plants learned to communicate in this way, an extraordinary interaction began. The plants now love playing with musical scales and making their own music with the help of a synthesizer.

The normally conservative world of science has also begun to explore plant consciousness. In February 2012, scientists at Exeter University demonstrated on film how plants warn each other of danger. When bugs or slugs attack a plant it gives off a special gas. Neighbouring plants pick this up and change their bio-chemical signals to keep the predator away. I expect those are only the physical signs of a much more subtle communication that's always going on in the plant world.

In *The Jaguar That Roams the Mind* Robert Tindall quotes the shaman Juan Flores Salazar as saying, 'The spirits of plants move about the world talking with one another, and if you connect sincerely with them, they teach this art. For a shaman, plants sustain life... plants with their roots in the soil and their branches spreading to the sky act as bridges between the worlds.'

In a strange combination of the old and new, to boost seed vitality for agriculture, China now uses 'super psychics'. They go into a deep trance and communicate with the seeds to produce plants that are healthier, faster growing and more fertile. And it works – the psychics can get seeds to sprout in minutes rather than days.

But you don't have to be a super psychic to help your garden grow. In *The Field* and *The Intention Experiment* Lynne McTaggart explains how physical reality is unified by an interactive field that can be affected by anyone's thoughts.

She did some experiments to prove this. In a web-based seminar, participants from all over the country sent their thoughts to a leaf – and successfully got it to glow for ten minutes. In another trial, people's thoughts encouraged a group of seeds to grow significantly faster and more robustly than the control sample.

These and many other scientific tests have fully established that plants not only have consciousness but can also hear us telepathically. They react strongly to good or bad thoughts that are sent to them – even from a distance.

'Nature is alive and is talking to us. This is not a metaphor,' said anthropologist Terence McKenna.

Zack, who in his regression recalled a life as an African shaman, described how he was trained to use this knowledge:

I've been taught how to speak with stones. I'm now learning how to speak to the water, the wind and the fire and how to ask them to work together.

There are ways to ask them to do things that are not part of the natural laws. But we can only do that if it's for the good of the land and if the nature gods agree to it.

Water can be persuaded to come out of the river and flow across the land to trees or plants or animals that need it. And in return the animals and the trees will help me in my work and protect me.

For our ancestors, being able to commune with nature was taken for granted. It was their common sense. After being derided for centuries, those ways are now turning out to be based on truth.

RESTORING YOUR PSYCHIC LINK WITH NATURE

Time spent in natural surroundings is always helpful – it refreshes the body, soothes the mind and invigorates the spirit. This tree meditation will enhance those effects in ways that are simple, safe and fun.

◉ Find a tree that you like and feel good about. Stand close to it, lean against it or sit under it. Put the palm of one or both of your hands on it. Then quieten your thoughts. Breathe slowly for a while, listening to the sound of your breath.

◉ When you feel ready, ask the tree to please send you healing, wholeness and inner strength. You can say this quietly in your mind, in a whisper or out loud – the spirit of the tree will hear you whichever way you choose.

- Then visualize beautiful colours and light flowing from the tree through your hands and filling your body.

- Feelings, images or impressions may also come into your mind. When a friend who was going through a difficult time did this, she felt that the tree was giving her its gift of endurance – the ability to withstand rough weather without being dismayed and bounce back again afterwards. She kept a solid twig from that tree to hold whenever she felt wobbly, and said it gave her real help. Your tree will also be happy to let you take whatever bits of it have fallen to the ground, so that you can stay connected to it even at a distance.

- When you feel ready to go, thank the tree and say goodbye.

You can go back to the tree and repeat this exercise whenever you wish. When you do, in its own way your special tree will recognize you, and the beneficial bond between you will strengthen.

As you do this, you may also start remembering the past lives when you had this forgotten birthright – humanity's ancient telepathic connection with nature.

4

HERBAL POWERS

One of my regression clients, Naomi, recalled a life as a tribal medicine woman in Europe after the fall of Rome. Invaders had moved into her area and claimed it for themselves. Naomi said once they'd built their fort and settled down, they started consulting her and taking her advice, but later they turned against her.

This kind of uneasy relationship between occupying powers and local magicians was fairly typical. Ancient Romans used to call on the fabled magic powers of the Sabines and the Etruscans to find hidden springs, bring rain or get messages from the dead. Even dignified Roman generals consulted Veleda, a famous seer of the Rhineland Bructei tribe. After the Normans invaded Britain, they called on witches to help them hunt down the rebel leader Hereward the Wake.

Naomi felt that it would protect her little tribe if she maintained an alliance with the people of the fort. But for unknown reasons, their initial friendliness had cooled off. So when she discovered a secret plot against them, she decided to warn them about it. This might put her back into favour and keep her tribe safe again.

She walked a long way through rough country and tangled woods to get to the fort. On the way, she saw a village that had been burnt down. It was a stark reminder of the kind of danger her people were facing.

Once she reached the fort, there was a new problem. She had once been able to come and go freely, but now the guard barred her entry.

After some thought, she decided to use one of her powers to get in. With the help of a potent herbal potion she would make herself look like something else:

> *I'll try it now. I can feel myself trying to slide past him – facing him but sort of gliding. Yes... it's working... I'm going past him and he isn't stopping me.*
>
> *I think he's not actually aware of me. I've become like a shadow passing. It's getting dark and I've sort of slipped past him like that.*

This description sounds more like a form of telepathic influence than literal shapeshifting.

A few years ago one of my clients, Lita, had an unexpected similar experience. Before going to work one morning, she went into deep meditation on the past-life dream she'd had the night before. Her former self had curly blonde hair done up in an ancient Grecian style which was quite different from Lita's long dark hair. This past self had important gifts to share: an easy sense of self-worth and gentle living from a time when goddesses were honoured as highly as gods. So, during her meditation, Lita allowed this former self to merge with her and become a part of her again. Then, suddenly realizing how late it was, she hurried off to work.

On the way, she felt a bit hurt when a friend walked straight past without greeting her, but she was soon at work, where she and a fellow employee always began the day with coffee and a cherry Danish pastry. That morning, though, he just glanced at her and then turned away.

By lunch-time he was friendly again, so she asked why he'd ignored her earlier. To her surprise, he said that he'd seen a blonde woman he didn't know sitting in her place.

For a short time after her meditation, Lita must have been unconsciously projecting the image of her former self. At the fort, Naomi probably did something similar – but more knowledgably, and with the help of some herbs.

Once Naomi had used her change of appearance to slip into the fort, she saw that a big feast was being prepared for important visitors. She knew these were the people who were plotting against their hosts, so she stopped one of the men and told him that these guests were really secret enemies.

This didn't go down at all well. They threw her into a small room and locked the door.

They don't trust me. They've shut me in here to put me out of the way. They think that I'm probably quite evil, and that I'm a witch. And that I can do horrible things to them.

They're suspicious of me because they trust these people and don't realize they are going to be a threat to them.

I don't know what to do. This window is too narrow.

When she said that, I thought she meant too narrow to climb out, but she meant that it was too narrow for a bird to come and carry a message back to her people.

Then the guards came back and dragged her out of the cell. She shrank in fear, expecting a beating. But they just laughed at her and then threw her out.

After this rough treatment, Naomi gave up trying to help them. Tired and hungry, she made the long journey home through dense woodlands and over rocky hills.

*I'm coming round the side of the hill now... and there is my
home. It's a small settlement... a lot of round houses... different
sizes. I can see drying animal skins. We turn them into coats
and use them to keep the huts warm. My children are running
to meet me. We are so happy to see each other again.*

*The warriors are all away. We don't know where they are or
what's happened to them. It's disturbing, but there's nothing
I can do about that now. I have things to see to – medicines
to make.*

AF: *What do you make them out of?*

N: *Herbs. I make different mixtures. There are dangers with
the herbs, though. We have to use them carefully. If you know
how to mix them properly, you can use medicines to rid people
of bad spirits. When the men are going into battle we make
potions from the forest herbs to give them courage.*

AF: *Do you do any other kind of magic?*

N: *Yes. We have special rituals to protect us and bring good
fortune, and there are the big celebrations when the seasons
change. At those times we dance and thank the gods for
everything.*

Healing of the Spirit

All shamanic healing first seeks the source of a problem
within the person's inner spirit, or psyche. Once that is cured,
the outer symptoms will clear up. For centuries medical
men have disregarded that way in favour of a physical-only
approach. But our world is now starting to understand
much more about how closely the mind, emotions and body
are woven together.

This was common sense for Elya in her past life as a
hermit. She said it felt as though it was very long ago and

perhaps somewhere like Wales – green, hilly and damp. People came to her for healing.

'I lay them on a bed made of herbs,' she said. 'They sleep on it and absorb the herbs through their skin. While that's happening I do things with their sleep. I see the sickness in their dreams and change it there.'

Shamans have always treated people's maladies with a combination of spiritual psychology and expert herbalism. They work with the spirit of the herb as much as its leaves and roots.

Mexican shaman Arbolita Pashak explained, 'Each *curandera*, healer, shaman, has a special plant with which they work. The plant and the healer work as one. We can establish a relation with the plants and the beings or spirits that live in them. We open to the information they have for us, opening to the transformation taking place inside them as a reflection of the transformation taking place in the universe.'

Herbal knowledge is the most ancient form of healing and has been used world-wide since prehistoric times. This wisdom was wiped out in the West first through the hysteria about witchcraft and then by the so-called Age of Reason. Within just a few centuries, traditional wise women and their valuable knowledge disappeared.

Or that's how it seems. I'm convinced that many of those women have reincarnated to continue their mission here. People often return to resume their long-term studies and share their learning with the world. The current resurgence of interest in natural medicine could well indicate that there's been a baby boom of ancient herbalists coming back.

Walking among us again may be monks and nuns from medieval herb gardens, the Persian and Arabian traders who brought herbal knowledge from the East, and, of course, the countless shamans and healers who lived outside the walls of recorded history. Many of these people have reincarnated at this time with the express purpose of bringing ancient knowledge back into the modern world. Perhaps you're one of them? If you feel attracted to herbalism, you might have past-life expertise to draw on – and the chance to share it with the world again.

5

ANIMAL MAGIC

Shamans traditionally have power animals as their messengers and guides. When a spirit animal becomes their ally, it increases their inner power. This gives extra protection from illness, attacks and misfortune in general.

Although it was usually only the shaman who had power animals, in that world everyone could commune with the animal kingdom and understand its messages.

When she was locked up in the fort, Naomi thought about sending a message home with a bird. She said birds made the best messengers, especially crows or rooks. If she was lucky, sometimes a squirrel or a fox would help out.

'I don't think they do it so much as the spirit that I ask to work through them,' she explained.

Since shamanic times, the language of animals has become a lost secret – but it can be learned again. As Billie later realized, the crows that appeared on the morning of her Native American workshop were bringing her a clear message.

Another of my clients, Brian, sent me this e-mail:

I have seen a large bird of prey circling above me,
silhouetted in exactly the same position, numerous times
in the past few weeks. The frequency and the fact it looks
like exactly the same bird, over and over, often hundreds
of miles apart, has made me think there may be some
significance to it... I would love your insights on this...

Brian had recently had a regression in which he had accessed the consciousness of his higher self. He'd felt as if he'd become tall and ethereal. A path of light had opened up before him, which he had followed, and he had soon found himself speeding through a vast multi-dimensional universe. He had seen many things, but too quickly to understand what they were.

He had received the message that he'd originally come from 'the place of the diamonds', but it wasn't yet time for him to fully understand what that meant. He'd been told this simply to reassure him that he had a high spiritual nature and a special path ahead.

After the regression he felt a bit dazed. He said he wished he could have some sort of proof that it was all true. Soon afterwards he wrote to me about the remarkable bird sightings he'd had.

Powerful birds can symbolize the ability to fly high above the world - just as Brian had done when he felt as if he was flying through great vistas of space and time. I felt that the mysterious bird he'd seen was a special sign, sent to him because he wanted reassurance about the messages he'd received during his regression.

INTERPRETING ANIMAL SIGNS AND SYMBOLS

The animal world sends us messages, warnings or encouragement in the form of signs and symbols. Like Brian's bird of prey, these animals or birds may be confirming something we've been wondering about or dispelling unnecessary doubts and worries.

You can identify a sign from the animal kingdom because it will stand out in some way. Not every animal you see in passing is a personal sign, but you'll know when you do see one. It will feel special – as if it's meant for you.

- ◎ If you want to find out more about the meaning, first look up what the animal symbolizes. Each animal stands for more than one quality, so you'll need to decide which aspect applies to your particular sighting.

- ◎ The next step is to consider what the animal means to you. These experiences are always personal, so it's helpful to go beyond the general symbolism. Thinking about the following questions will give you some good clues:

  - ◊ What memories or associations do you have concerning that animal?

  - ◊ What did other elements about the sighting remind you of?

  - ◊ How did it make you feel?

  - ◊ If the scene had been in a movie, what would it mean?

  - ◊ Where were you going to or coming from at the time?

  - ◊ What was the main thing on your mind?

- ◎ You can also tune in to the animal by focusing on its image in your mind's eye. Ask what its message is for you and trust that an answer will come – if not straight away, perhaps as a sudden realization later on.

- ◎ Another good method is to ask for the meaning of the sign to come to you in a dream. Even if you don't recall the dream, the answer could surface into your mind within a few days.

These experiences not only give us useful messages and advice, they also help to wake up our old magical awareness, reminding us that all life on this planet is connected – not only physically but also spiritually.

The Great Bear Spirit

One morning, having coffee in one of Glastonbury's cafés, I was introduced to Andy. When he heard that I did past-life regression, he told me about a strange memory that had come to him during meditation.

He had found himself in a world that he described as 'dark, northern, mysterious and magical'. In the woods there was a bear that had become a source of great fear in his home village.

> I set off on a quest to conquer it. I camped out in a tent of some kind. It was winter, so I hoped the bear would be hibernating and I'd catch it napping. But in the middle of the night it came to me. It was such a shock that it sent me into a kind of altered reality.
>
> At first, I was completely terrified. Then I surrendered to it. It wasn't just 'OK, you win, you can kill me', it was as if I suddenly appreciated it more fully – I accepted it and its power.
>
> And it spared me – I wasn't killed. I went back to the village to tell them the bear had let me live, rather than the other way round, as intended.

Andy asked if I could help him find out more about this. So a few days later I put him into a deeply relaxed state with the suggestion that he connect to a spirit guide to discover more about this episode.

His guide told him that he'd accessed only the most dramatic part of a much bigger memory. The bear encounter had been part of an ongoing process of shamanic initiation for him.

For the rest of that life, he'd followed a path of learning about the magic of the Earth. The memory had returned to him now to prompt him about inner powers that he had but feared - and needed to accept again.

The next time I bumped into Andy he told me he'd decided to make use of his guide's advice by getting into bears:

> I started collecting pictures and models of them and connecting with the Great Bear Spirit in meditation. This got me doing all kinds of psychic stuff I would never have done otherwise - shamanic journeying, that sort of thing. And I'm loving it. The bear spirit really is helping me to find my inner powers.

The Secret Life of Pets

I once lived with a man who had a grey cat called Mothy. One day she disappeared. We looked everywhere, but had to give up in the end.

About a week later, Mothy came to me in a dream. She let me know that she'd moved on to the next world and had come to say goodbye and thanks for everything.

When I told my partner this dream, he looked visibly shaken. I asked him what the matter was - and he said that the previous night he'd had exactly the same dream.

Mothy had found a way to send her message to us both at the same time. Since then, I've been much more aware of the ongoing telepathic connection we always have with our pets.

Pets can also reincarnate to be with us again. About a year after her dear old dog Paddy had died, my friend

Elvira dreamed that he was back and happily sleeping in his basket again.

A few months later, she was given a new puppy. She said although she didn't want to believe it at first, she became convinced this puppy was Paddy reincarnated:

> Whenever Paddy wanted to go for a walk, he used to sit and gaze at the lead that hangs on the wall. Every so often he'd turn round and give us a beseeching look. The new puppy began to do exactly the same thing, even before we'd put the lead on him! He also has the same favourite foods and toys as Paddy. It feels exactly like Paddy is back with us – and he's so happy to be here again.

And it's not just pets. In *The Case for Reincarnation*, Joe Fisher said that jockey Steve Donaghue was convinced that the Tetrarch, one of the fastest horses in history, had lived before as a racehorse.

'From the day he had the breaking tack on, he knew his business,' said the jockey. 'He knew everything there was to know about racing the first time I took him onto a course.'

The Lion Queen

Our psychic connection with the animal kingdom may be one of our greatest natural gifts. Many people have experienced magical encounters in the wild and had telepathic exchanges with rescue animals or pets. Science, however, turns up its collective nose at anecdotal data. The rule is, if it can't be tested in a laboratory, it can't be proved and therefore isn't real. As a result, our ancient link with the animal kingdom has been shut outside the parameters of accepted mainstream belief. But now and then a tale emerges that's not so easy to ignore.

In 1991 a small group of tourists in South Africa experienced dramatic proof of the power of animal telepathy. Linda Tucker was touring Timbavati Game Reserve with her husband and friends when their Land Rover broke down. Night was falling. A hungry pride of lions began to close in around them. In panic, they started screaming for help.

Then Linda saw what looked like a strange ghost coming towards them out of the darkness. It turned out to be an old woman with a baby on her back and two youngsters holding on to her from behind. They were shuffling along in a trance-like state. The woman was murmuring a sing-song chant over and over. She was the shaman Maria Khosa, otherwise known as the Lion Queen of Timbavati. As she drew near, the lions quietened down.

The lions trusted Maria. So at her request they held off and allowed one of the tourists to go and get help for the rest of the party.

When she had heard the cries for help, Maria said she had first called on the ancestors for guidance. Then she had entered *twasa* – the hypnotic trance that all shamans use for their work. In this state, she had been able to communicate with the lions and persuade them to leave the people in the Land Rover in peace.

Our psychic contact with animals may have grown weak through lack of use. But I think it's a natural human ability and brimming with positive future potential.

If you love animals, or work with them, you may find it easy to communicate with them telepathically – especially if this is one of your past-life skills. You might even discover an old friend. I'm convinced that animals reincarnate and recognize people they were close to in former lives.

When enough people remember these old ways I believe that humanity will once again be able to talk – and listen – to animals.

DEVELOPING TELEPATHY WITH ANIMALS

If you'd like to develop your natural telepathy with animals, here are some tips to help you on your way:

- Animals are always using telepathy and extra-sensory perception – it's normal for them. They send and receive feelings, images and impressions. Our brain translates those messages into words. So, the best way to send animals (and people!) a telepathic message is to combine your words with images and feelings.

- Start with your pets when you're at home. Send them loving thoughts to open the telepathic connection between you. Then practise sensing their thoughts and feelings.

- Repeat these steps when you're away from them.

- When you feel ready, do the same with other animals, starting with those in your immediate surroundings.

- The next step is tuning in to animals that are far away. People who've developed this skill may receive inspiring messages from whales and dolphins, for example.

- One of the best ways to use this ability is to send reassurance to animals that are upset or frightened – you can do that even from a great distance.

- As you go along, the animal kingdom will respond by sending you interesting experiences to confirm and develop your skill. A fascinating adventure of exploration will unfold!

❖ ❖ ❖

6

FLYING

The most important skill shamans have is the ability to fly to other realms for answers and cures to help their people. This is so key that cave art and ancient petroglyphs from all over the world depict shamans in flight.

Shamanic initiation trains them where to go on these journeys, how to get there and how to avoid the dangers. The shaman is taught how to travel from the 'middle world' we live in to the 'lower world' of nature magic, the 'upper world' of higher spirit and all kinds of parallel 'middle worlds'.

In his regression Zack described how he was trained to go to the upper world in his preparation to be an African shaman:

I'm learning to fly to the stars. I go through special places in the Earth – places of power. They say one day I'll learn to fly with my physical body as well, not just the spirit body.

They've taught me how to fly to a special star. It's where my people came from very long ago. I don't go there directly – there are lots of junctions. The pathways turn and twist. I go there at great speed. That place has many different types of creatures and beings living on it. Some of them are very large.

Afterwards I come back and tell my teachers what I've seen. They'll know if I really went there because of how I describe it.

Shapeshifting

Towards the end of Naomi's regression, she talked about another way of flying: shapeshifting. To do this, shamans must first seek out the oversoul of a power animal. When they find one that is happy to work with them, it becomes their personal symbol and can be their double when needed.

To fly or travel in other realms, the shaman becomes their power animal. This might be via astral projection, with the shaman's spirit body clothed in the form of the power animal. Even so, according to legends and personal accounts, these exploits are definitely physical. If, during a mission, the double is hurt or killed, the shaman will fall ill or die soon after.

Here are Naomi's memories of that experience:

Winter's coming now. It's getting towards the end of the year and there's still no news of our warriors. Where are they? They should have been back by now. It's been too long. No messengers have come. None of my bird messages have come back. This is work I'm going to have to do myself. I must set off on my travels again. But this time I want to fly.

AF: *Can you fly?*

N: *Not often. For me, it only works when there's a very strong reason for it – when there's no other way left. This is how it is now. So I've gone to a place far from the settlement, where nobody can see me. I'm asking the spirits of the birds, the* *spirits of the air, to help me in my quest. And then... just... it's working! I'm in the air.*

AF: *How did you do it?*

N: *I sort of jumped... and now I'm a bird. It just happens. I don't know how. I don't know what kind of bird I am. I have brown feathers. I feel quite strong. I can feel myself moving against the wind, sometimes pushing against it. It buffets me, but I keep going quite steadily. I can sometimes float on it.*

The landscape beneath me is very clear. I can see everything in great detail. There are many trees – the forest is very dense. The leaves are yellow and red now. There's open land as well. I'm ranging quite far... searching... searching...

(Long pause)

I can't find them anywhere. I must go back.

Going back... going back... going down. I'm dropping rapidly from a great height, but there's no feeling of my stomach falling. It feels completely smooth.

My feet touch the ground. I'm still a bird. I'm standing up. And I'm a human.

After the regression, Naomi said that even as a memory the flight was an amazing experience. She had the strong impression that it was not out-of-body travel. The physical feelings were so vivid and real, she was convinced she really had shapeshifted into a bird in order to fly.

Folklore and religious records from all over the world are full of reports about people who could fly. Irish legends say the Druids were powerful magicians who could change themselves into any shape they chose, while Hindu, Christian and Islamic writings all describe the physical levitations of saints and mystics.

The *Rig-Veda* talks about magicians flying around during the night 'like birds'. Hindu *sadhus* (gurus) are all expected to have the *siddhi* (power) of levitation as a natural outcome of their spiritual development.

The yogi Subbayah Pullaver used to lie down, go into a deep trance and then levitate horizontally several feet above the ground. In 1936 he did this in front of 150 witnesses.

The seventeenth-century Italian priest Joseph of Copertino was called 'the Flying Monk' because in moments of religious joy he physically rose into the air, sometimes drifting along for a fair distance. He did this often, especially during services. In the course of his life, countless numbers of startled church-goers witnessed his flights.

The nineteenth-century medium Daniel Dunglass Home was able to levitate both himself and heavy pieces of furniture. Crowds of people watched in broad daylight as he flew out of one third-storey window and in at another. He could also make himself several inches taller at will and often floated up to the ceiling. Committees of determined sceptics tested him dozens of times, but could never manage to disprove his powers.

Other famous names said to have been able to fly were the ancient Greek philosopher Apollonius of Tyana, the Gnostic Simon Magus, the Christian saints Francis of Assisi and Teresa of Avila, and Ignatius Loyala, founder of the Jesuits.

But flying wasn't only for mystics or magicians. Before the Church finally managed to stamp out shamanic herbal potions, ordinary people flew with the help of flying ointment.

The complete recipe for this has been lost – or else is being kept very secret. We know it had an oil or grease base, to which was added some careful doses of strong poisons from plants such as wolfsbane, hemlock and deadly nightshade.

The ointment was then rubbed on the body, especially in areas where it could be absorbed easily. This probably explains the tales of witches flying astride their broomsticks.

As part of its campaign against the old ways, the Church spread the rumour that flying ointment was made from the fat of an unbaptized child. This demonized those who used it and put off those who hadn't tried it yet. As a result, tales of flying ointment are now just whispers from the past.

It may look as though the doors of magical flight have been closed to us; however, in recent decades a completely new way of flying has begun to emerge. In the 1970s Robert Monroe opened the path of astral travel to everyone with his riveting books about out-of-body experiences. He later established the Monroe Institute, so that anyone could learn this skill. Since then the subject has blossomed, with a steady stream of books and articles being published and workshops on offer. With so much information about conscious astral travel now widely available, it's no longer necessary to risk the dangers of physical levitation.

In times of natural magic, it was taken for granted that every shaman knew how to fly. In the future, it may be just as acceptable for everyone to travel freely in their spirit body. The ancient way of the shaman may one day become the natural way for all of us.

7

THE BRIDGE TO THE OTHER WORLD

One of the greatest legacies to us from shamanic times is a positive view of death. In those days, death simply meant that the spirit left the body and moved on to the next world. Journeys to those realms and visits from them were part of everyday life. The 'other side' was not only real, it was familiar.

How different this is from the established beliefs of the western world. For centuries, the Church threatened people with the prospect of hellfire and damnation after death. For many, the only alternative to this was the 'rational' belief that we are nothing but bodies and death is the end of all consciousness.

Those beliefs have warped our lives and spoiled our deaths. Difficult deaths create all kinds of neuroses and phobias in subsequent lives. Much of regression therapy today is spent undoing those effects. With less fear, the experience would be much more peaceful. People would know how to simply slip out of the body, even if death came in a sudden or violent way.

Dr Helen Wambach said, 'It's quite common for my subjects to tell me after they've experienced death in a past-life regression that a phobia or symptom they had has gone away.'

How did we come to forget the wise old ways? In 2005 Dr Nigel Spivey presented a BBC mini-series called *Death in Art*, showing how the fear of death had been used as a means of control from Aztec times to the present day. He explained how images of death had the power to bind people to a cause. Pictures of enemies slain by your leaders are reassuring in one way, because it means you're on the victorious side. But they hold a sinister sub-text: toe the line or the same thing could happen to you.

When it's been stirred up, fear of death makes people more partisan. They feel growingly threatened by groups that are different from their own. This supports social hierarchies and reinforces the power of the state. It also drives people to war.

In huge contrast, the shamanic view of death is that it's a natural process, not an enemy to be feared. It comes when it's meant to – when the soul knows it's time to move on. Old age, sickness or accidents don't 'cause' it. Those are just doors that it uses.

For those who live close to nature, death is simply part of the ever-changing cycle of life. The sun may seem to die at the end of the day, but it lives again in the morning. The landscape looks dead in winter, but life returns in spring. These everyday miracles hold important messages for us about the true nature of life and death.

The Boat Across the Lake

One of my regression clients recalled a life as a Native American. In her old age, she knew it was nearly time to go. She prepared for it peacefully.

When she finally floated out of her body, she saw a huge lake. A boat was coming across it to fetch her. After a last look back at the mountains she loved, she got into the boat.

She knew she was going to a place of peace and safety where she could recover from her physical sojourn and think about what to do next.

Mission Complete

Kass, the wise woman of the woodland tribe, said that she was ready to leave that life once she'd completed her mission. With her sisters, she'd trained a new younger wise woman to guide the tribe. She felt that she'd be leaving her people in good hands.

They had a major ceremony to mark the inauguration of the new wise woman:

> We made a big circle inside the stones. We did the old rituals to bring our gods into the stone circle. And they came.

> When that was finished, we told the tribe it was time for them to have a new wise woman, a young one, who would bring in a new time for them. Then we uncloaked her and brought her forward.

> It was a big surprise to them. The secret had been kept well. She looked so beautiful in her special robes. The whole tribe stared at her open-mouthed.

> She spoke to them with a strong and clear voice. She told them that in a vision she'd seen our people moving through a world of mud and wind and dark: 'But we are heading for a beautiful summer land. It'll be a place filled with wonders. Our gods and spirits will lead us there. This night is the start of the journey to our summer land.'

After that everyone danced and sang. My sisters and I watched for a while. Our hearts were full of joy. Then we left them and walked back. Our work was done.

My life was then complete. I could stop holding the shadows of death at bay. I lay down and allowed them to flood into my body. Soon afterwards I became ill. But it was a gentle illness. There was little pain. My sisters tended me with great care. While I lay ill, the people left many tributes at the door.

I slowly drifted away. Little by little, the spirits of the forest began to take me with them. One day I went off with them completely and never returned.

Practising before Departure

In Zack's life as an African shaman he became familiar with the other realms long before it was time for him to move there. Here he describes one of those experiences:

I reach out for the spirit being who will give me the best advice. Then I let myself be drawn to the place where that spirit is. It feels like going very fast through a tunnel.

It's taken me to a very big place. I recognize it. I've met wise guides here before. I wait in the big round open area in the middle. Many passages lead off it.

Someone is coming through one now. It's a very large being. It looks as if he wears billowing blue robes, but the robes are really his own light. He comes to me and stands before me. I don't have to speak; he can see what I want to know.

When it was time for Zack to leave that life, it was easy – he simply went the way he'd always gone to get guidance from the spirits.

I was content in that life. But just the same, when it was time to go, I was pleased. I was quite old by then – older than most of the tribe. I hadn't been feeling well for a while. So I decided this would be a good time to go. I didn't want to become so old and ill that people would have to look after me for a long time.

I retired to my hut and went in and out of the dream state for several days, communing with the gods and spirits. One day I went through the tunnel again, but this time much more slowly. I was floating for a while, like a leaf on a stream. It felt wonderful.

After a while I saw a light and went towards it. When I got there, I found the ancestors waiting for me. I knew then that I wouldn't be going back again.

They took me to their beautiful place of learning. I stayed there for a long time, learning many more things before I was ready for another Earth life.

A New Bridge

The culture that we live in does much to shape our expectations about death. Charon ferried the souls of ancient Greeks over the river Styx. Anubis took ancient Egyptians to the underworld. Norse people flew to Asgard – unless they'd died in battle, in which case the Valkyries flew them to the Halls of Valhalla.

These tales act like well-trodden pathways from this world to the next, making it easier for the soul to leave the physical world. Some would say our culture no longer has any useful symbolic bridges to the other side, but I think it has. A powerful new bridge is being built by all the people who've had near-death experiences and survived to tell the tale.

Many have validated these experiences by accurately reporting things they saw and heard while floating above their apparently dead body. With mass printing and the power of the internet, these accounts have spread throughout the world.

They all describe much the same thing. After leaving the body, the person hovers above it for a while to watch what's happening – feeling completely detached about the outcome. Then a tunnel opens up. A beautiful light draws them through it, with a wonderful sense of love and peace. When they reach the light, they encounter spirit guides or loved ones. They often receive inspiring messages.

Finally they're told to go back – it isn't their time to come here. They all say how disappointing it is to hear that. Afterwards, many of them make major positive changes in their lives, with spiritual values at the centre. Their books, articles and interviews are helping to transform everyone's understanding of what lies beyond this life.

Discovering past lives is another good way to do that. Whether we recall one or several lives, it becomes clear that the spirit never dies. In recent years, following the ground-breaking work of Dr Michael Newton, an exciting new development has emerged: memories of the between-life worlds. With that gate now open, it's become easier for people to access those experiences. This has become another good source of information and reassurance about the afterlife.

Simply believing in reincarnation makes a big difference. After the terrible Indian Ocean tsunami in 2004, surveys were conducted to assess how the survivors' belief systems had helped them. It turned out that those who believed in reincarnation were more resilient and recovered more quickly than those who didn't.

When the fear of death withers away, so do all its spin-off anxieties and harmful side-effects.

'The unresolved trauma of death is a primary cause of behavioural disorder,' said Dr Morris Netherton. 'Most of the problems I encounter have their source in past-life deaths; when the impact of these deaths is erased, many disorders simply evaporate.'

Returning to our past-life shamanic wisdom about the true nature of death will foster lives of peace and hope instead of fear and guilt. As this awareness spreads, it will create a firm foundation for a happier and more peaceful world in the future.

VISITING THE TEMPLE OF WISDOM AND HEALING

This is an immense place on the higher astral plane. It has vast libraries and many different areas where you can receive guidance, knowledge or inner healing. You can go there whenever you wish in meditation or the dream state.

It can also be a beautiful bridge to the other world. For departing spirits who have become familiar with it during their lives, it provides a clear path to the higher realms and a safe haven for rest and recuperation.

◎ When you wish to visit the temple, first decide on the purpose of your journey. It needn't be for anything specific – you can go there simply to enjoy the environment and soak up the beneficial atmosphere.

◎ Ask your guardian angel or favourite spirit guide to take you there. We all have these helpers and they assist whenever we ask – even if we're not always aware of it.

◎ You may then feel as if angel wings have wrapped around you to fly you straight up a tube of light directly to the higher astral planes.

- Once there, you'll see the Temple of Wisdom and Healing set in beautiful surroundings. Go up the steps to the wide-open doors and into a huge entrance hall. A temple guide will welcome you warmly, offer to show you around or take you to the area that best suits the purpose of your visit.

- When you feel ready to leave, your guardian angel or spirit guide will take you safely back.

- Once home again, send thanks to all who helped you.

You can return whenever you wish. The more you go there, the easier it will become to access all that the temple has to offer.

8

GIFTS FROM THE PAST

Past-life influences can surface from any era to help us solve a current life issue. Whatever our past selves may have been through, with the strengths and understanding they gained, they can become real allies to us. This is especially true of our shamanic past lives, which so often remind us of key spiritual knowledge and forgotten inner powers.

The Watcher

When Mel came for a regression, his life was heading for a crisis. Family and financial worries were snapping at his heels. Dogged by sleepless nights, he began to wonder if his problems came from a former life. To his surprise, he accessed a past life that, instead of being the source of his problems, helped him to solve them.

The first impressions he had were of open countryside. It was windswept, scrubby and sparse. He was a boy of about 17. The wind was cold and he was dressed in warm, furry clothes. Alone out there, he was a watcher for his tribe.

Although seldom seen, there were bands of marauders out there. They could strike without mercy. If Mel saw any sign of other people in that vast empty plain, his duty was to leap on his horse and race back to warn his people.

They were a nomadic tribe, used to moving on. The grass was poor and they always needed to find new places with fresh grass for their horses and goats.

He enjoyed being a watcher:

I love being alone out here. When I'm here the spirits speak to me – spirits of the wind... and the earth. Sometimes the wind blows into my mind in a special way. When it does that, pictures come into my mind.

Sometimes I see people in my mind that are too far away to see with my eyes. I can tell if they're coming towards us or not. So the spirits help me to watch. They protect us.

Once I was shown a nice green valley we could go to, with lots of grass for our animals. I told the elders about that. We went there and it was true.

Lately they've been showing me other things – things I don't want to see. They say that soon I mustn't come out here and listen to them anymore. That makes me sad.

The sun is setting now. It's time for me to return. I'm getting on my horse, going slowly back. The wind is blowing around me. I can feel it's trying to tell me something. But it's something I don't want to know.

He went back to the camp, where he stayed in the watchers' tent. He told me more about his life:

When boys are about 12 years old, they have to move from their families to this big tent and become watchers. There's a woman here who cooks food for us and makes sure we do our work.

*She's very strong and wise in her spirit. When a boy knows
what work he wants to do, he moves on from this place to begin
his new training. Some of them only stay here for a short time.*

AF: *What sort of work do they choose?*

M: *Warriors. Hunters. Making things. Tending the animals.*

AF: *What will you do?*

M: *This is the problem: I don't know. I like being a watcher,
but I can't choose that.*

AF: *Why not?*

M: *It's boys' work. If I don't choose my real work soon, people
will say I'm not a real man. Even the girl that I like now
spends more time with my friend. She said I'm turning into
a ghost. They laugh at me behind my back. If I don't decide
what to do soon, others will also start laughing at me. But
there's nothing else that I want to do.*

In the next development, he found himself in the chief's
tent with the shaman and other elders. He was on a kind
of trial. He'd told a little girl a fairy story that he thought
would give her courage after her parents had fallen ill and
died. The elders heard about it and were deciding whether it
was a good or bad thing to do. But he felt that what he was
really on trial for was his delay in taking up a man's work.

AF: *What was the story about?*

M: *About a little girl, like her, who was chosen by the spirits
to go on a difficult journey. I told her about all the difficult
things that little girl had to face and how she overcame
them all – how her courage grew. At the end of the journey
she turned into something like a princess and was greatly
honoured by everyone.*

That was the story. I thought it would help, that's all. I wish I hadn't done it now. I have enough problems in my life, without this as well.

The elders are talking quietly to each other. Sometimes they ask the girl questions. The shaman doesn't say much. He keeps looking at me.

Now they say it's my turn to speak. The shaman says I must hold nothing back – I must tell everything that's in my heart.

So I tell them how I felt sorry for the child and why I thought that story would help. I tell them that I like being a watcher because I can hear the stories that the spirits give me. That's why I know that stories are good magic.

When I've told them everything in my heart, I stop.

They are all just looking at me. Nobody says anything. I don't know what to do.

Now the shaman is reminding the elders about that message I had that led us to the lush valley. We had some good summers there till the marauders kicked us out and took it over. The elders are nodding. They liked it there.

The shaman says I must go, so they can talk. I bow to them and go outside. I'm glad to be out of there. I don't have any duties today because of this trial, so I just wander around.

I go over to see where some boys who used to be watchers are being trained as warriors. They're learning how to fight on horseback. I can feel how excited they are. I wish I felt the same way. But even if I don't want to, I may have to join them if I don't choose my own path soon. The tribe always needs more warriors.

Here comes the shaman. The meeting must be over. He calls me to him. He says I must come to his tent. He has a lot to tell me. I'm so nervous.

Back in his tent, he says they decided the story I told was a good thing for the child, so I won't be punished. But I mustn't go around telling stories anymore. The same goes for my messages from the spirits, and my dreams. From now on I can only speak of these things to the shaman and he will decide what to do about them. Because of this, I must become his apprentice. If I don't want to do that, I must never again speak of stories or visions or dreams. That is their decree.

The shaman says he'll only take me on as an apprentice if I really want to do this work, because I'll have to be completely dedicated to it. He says it's not all nice stuff like listening to the spirits. I'll have to learn a lot of things. Some of them are quite difficult.

He says I must go away and think about it and give him my answer by nightfall.

AF: How do you feel about that?

M: Confused. Overwhelmed. To be chosen as the shaman's apprentice – even in this strange way – is a very great honour.

AF: Did you not consider this for your life's work before?

M: No. I never thought about it because it's up to the shaman to choose his apprentice. It's not something someone can just decide for himself. And I don't know if I can ever do the things he does.

AF: What does he do?

M: He heals all kinds of sicknesses and wounds and broken bones. He also does powerful magical chanting for the whole tribe. I don't think I'll ever be able to do that. I'll just make a big fool of myself. Then people really will be laughing at me.

I went back to the watchers' tent. The woman who looked after us had made a big pot of stew. I got a bowl of that and went outside to have it.

My friend Alu came along. He wasn't a watcher anymore and he looked down on me now, because we started being watchers at the same time and I'd been left behind.

He asked me in a mocking way why I wasn't out there watching, so I told him what'd been going on. And he laughed. He said I'd be a failure as the shaman's apprentice as well.

I went back into the watchers' tent and lay down on the sleeping furs. The woman who cooked for us asked why I was there, so I told her everything that'd happened – that Alu had said I'd fail as the shaman's apprentice and I thought he might be right.

She suddenly got very angry. She shouted so loudly, she woke up the other boys.

She yelled at me to stand up. She said it was the last time I'd ever lie down in that tent. I had to leave it forever because I was going to be the tribe's next shaman. I had to start that work that day.

Then she pushed me out and said I should never come back.

I didn't know what to do, so I went back to the shaman's tent. I found him sitting in the sun, mixing something in a bowl. I just stood there, not saying anything.

He told me to sit down next to him. Then he explained what he was mixing. It was some sort of medicine. He needed some extra little thing for it. He asked me to go and get it from inside his tent. So I did that.

He asked me to shred it up for him. I did that. Then he said he had to go and do something and while he was gone I had to mix it into the bowl. So I did that.

When he came back he looked at the mix and said I had just done my first job as his new apprentice.

Then he gave me another little job to do. He kept on doing that for the rest of the day.

When nightfall came, he asked what I'd decided. I said I'd accept the apprenticeship if he offered it, but I didn't think I'd ever have his powers.

He just laughed and said, 'You have now found your true work.'

The next key episode in that life took place some years later, when Mel was about 30.

I'm feeling very nervous. There's a big meeting with the whole tribe. The shaman has told me that after he's done his chanting, I have to stand up and speak. I have to talk to the whole tribe at once. I've never done that before. He says I must tell everyone about a dream I had.

AF: *Why does he want you to do that?*

M: *Because we have a big problem. It's what this meeting is about. It's to do with our horses. We have too many now. The horse is sacred to us. We won't drive a single one away. It's not like the goats – we will never eat our horses or use their milk or fur – so if we have too many we don't know what to do with them. And they eat too much of the grass, so we have to keep moving on more than we want to.*

I asked for an answer to this in a dream. When it came, I told it to the shaman. Now he says I must tell it to the whole tribe.

As evening falls, everyone starts to gather in a great circle. There's a big fire in the middle to keep us warm. We've brought the horses nearby, because this is about them. They're standing round the outer edges of the circle. Their eyes are shining in the firelight. I think their spirits understand what's going on.

The ceremonies begin. The shaman does his chants. I drum for him as usual. When he's finished he says I must stand up and speak.

I'm feeling very shaky. As I stand, I silently ask the spirits to be with me. Then I start to talk. Everyone goes quiet.

I tell them that I asked the spirits to send me an answer to our problem and the Great Horse Spirit spoke to me in a dream. It said if we let the horses lead the way, they'd show us to the solution.

The people start asking me, 'What will the answer be? Where will the horses lead us?' But I don't know the answers to their questions. I sit down again. I'm sure they think that wasn't a very good message.

Next day the elders had meetings about this with the shaman and they decided to try it out. They're going to do what the dream said: let the horses lead us to the solution. That means untying them and following where they go.

There's a ceremony before we go. The shaman asks the Great Horse Spirit to guide and help us. Then we set the horses free...

For a long time, they just carry on grazing nearby. But little by little they begin to move further away. We follow slowly behind.

That goes on for many days. The horses are moving in one general direction, but so slowly, stopping to graze a lot. The people are beginning to get impatient. They are turning against me, muttering that this is a stupid idea.

I wish the shaman would just call it off. I wish I'd never told him that dream. But he says we must keep going and be patient.

(Pause)

Things have just got worse. Yesterday one of the watcher boys came rushing back in a big panic. He'd seen another settlement in the distance – and said the horses were heading straight for it.

What an uproar that caused! Everyone started to say that the horses were leading us into danger, that my dreams came from bad spirits, that I couldn't be trusted.

The elders came to me. They asked if my dream said anything about this. It didn't. They said as I had started this, I had to do something now.

So I did the only thing I could think of: I went out onto the plains like I used to do when I was a watcher. I asked for the answer to come to me on the wind. Should we keep following the horses? And risk a battle with these other people?

The answer came: 'Keep going. All will be well.'

I went back and told the shaman what I'd got. He went off to speak with the elders about it. Now I'm standing alone, waiting for the elders' decision. Everyone is glaring at me.

(Pause)

The meeting is over. Here comes the shaman. His eyes are avoiding mine. I've never seen him look nervous before. This doesn't feel good.

He tells me that the elders have decided to keep following my vision. But if anything goes wrong, I will be stripped of

*my position as assistant shaman. I will never be allowed
to train for anything else either. I will become a pariah – a
disgraced person.*

AF: *What does that mean?*

M: *It's like being branded. If you stay with the tribe, for the
rest of your life you only do the dirty work. You are ignored by
the whole tribe. You become a non-person. If it turns out like
that, I will do the honourable thing.*

AF: *What is that?*

M: *To walk away and never return.*

AF: *Alone, into the wilderness?*

M: *Yes. Anyone who's been outcast in this way can choose
to remain in the tribe as a pariah, or can be remembered for
having done a final noble thing – walking away.*

AF: *Is anyone who walks away likely to survive alone out there?*

M: *No. This is why it's an honourable last act. It redeems
whatever mistake you made.*

*Now the advisors have told the people to keep going where the
horses lead. Everyone is starting to look frightened. If this goes
wrong, I can forget about any noble last act – these people
will take my death into their own hands.*

*The other settlement has come into view now. We stop. One
of the elders comes to me. He says I must go out there alone to
greet these strangers. If I don't return, they'll give me up and
flee from that place. So I'm preparing to do that.*

*The shaman is giving me lots of advice. I must go on foot,
because it looks more peaceful, and hold my hands out with
palms up, to show I have no weapons. I ask the spirits to be
with me. And I set out.*

As I get nearer, a small group of men comes from the camp, walking towards me. They're carrying spears, like warriors, but they're also on foot.

I hold out my hands to show that I have no weapons, and that I come in peace. When there's still quite a distance between us, they stop. So do I. I make a gesture of respect and bow.

One of the warriors steps forward. He starts to walk slowly towards me. I walk slowly towards him as well. We both stop when there's still a safe distance between us.

He calls out, 'What do your people want?'

I try to explain about the horses. It's difficult. He's listening with a frown. He keeps asking me to explain again. I'm sure he thinks this is a trick.

He goes back to the others. I can see him trying to tell them what I just said. I can feel how baffled and suspicious they are. They glance over their shoulders at me and then carry on jabbering to each other. I stand and wait. I look back to my own people. They're all standing watching in silence.

The warriors finish talking and the leader comes back to me. He says they are also peaceful people. Because of that, their leader will speak with our leader.

I go back with this news. There's great excitement about it. The elders start fussing around our leader, getting him ready. Then he sets out for the meeting with his retinue of advisors.

The two leaders meet on the open ground. Everyone is watching. I can feel how tense everyone is on both sides. Both are ready to strike at the slightest sign of anything wrong. I'm asking the spirits to keep things calm. I think the shaman is doing the same.

After what seems a very long time, our chief comes back to us. Everyone crowds around. He announces that those people don't want to fight us. Everyone cheers.

He says they were badly attacked by marauders a few years ago. They still haven't recovered. Nobody cheers about that, but there's a big feeling of relief. They aren't a threat to us.

The chief continues. Because of that attack, they lost many warriors. They also lost most of their horses. He pauses and looks around to let that sink in. Some of the people start to realize what this means: our extra horses suddenly aren't a problem anymore – they are something precious that we can trade or bargain with in some way.

Everyone is glancing at me in a new way. The shaman gives me a big nudge.

The chief tells us that those people know about a fertile valley with a river. They haven't gone there because they fear it will draw another attack to them. But if we band together and go there, we may be able to defend ourselves.

He stops talking. Everyone is silent, taking this in.

The shaman suddenly speaks up. He says, 'This means the vision was a true one. The Spirit of the Horses has guided us well!'

All the people start to cheer.

Now the chief asks the shaman and me to join him and the elders in their meeting to sort out all the details. It's such an honour for me.

Just before we go into that meeting, the shaman stops me and puts his hands on my shoulders. He looks intently into my eyes. Then he does some quiet chanting and rubs some stuff with his thumb onto my forehead.

AF: *Why does he do that?*

M: *He's giving me authority.*

AF: *What kind of authority?*

M: *To start taking his place as the shaman. He's quite old by now. He tells me that for a while he's wanted to retire and become a respected advisor to the chief, but he's been waiting for the right moment. Now that my horse dream has worked out, it's the perfect time. The people will accept me now.*

So before we moved to the new valley, we had a big ceremony and he made me the new shaman. It was the most wonderful moment of my life.

AF: *How did everything work out after that?*

M: *It went well. The two tribes benefited each other in so many ways. Much later marauders came and attacked us. They wanted our beautiful river valley. But by then we were a big and strong tribe, so we fended them off. After that, we stayed in that place. Life was good there.*

AF: *Why do you think this memory has come up for you now?*

M: *It was to remind me of how strong I became. After going through those tests, I felt that I could handle anything that life threw at me. I can tap into that again now. It will help me through my current problems.*

Afterwards I asked Mel where he thought this had taken place. He said it felt like somewhere in Central Asia, possibly Mongolia.

When I researched it later, I found that horse-riding nomads had roamed that area from prehistoric times. Later on, some of the tribes had started joining together to form powerful confederations.

In July 2012, some years after this regression took place, a group of scientists announced they'd discovered that ancient Mongols had invaded Eurasia mainly because they needed better grass for their horses. It was exactly the way of life that Mel had described – and I believed him when he said he'd never read a thing about this obscure corner of history.

I felt rather awed that a memory from so long ago had the power to reach across the centuries and restore the inner strength that Mel had forged in that life. It had been buried and forgotten and that memory was just what he needed to prod it awake again.

The next time I heard from him, a few months later, he said his life had begun to turn around. Everything was starting to look better. He was sure it was because he'd got a memory that reminded him to believe in himself, no matter how tough the trials of life might be.

As in Mel's case, our past selves can bring gifts to us in the form of reminders to believe in ourselves, our purpose and our inner guidance. They can also help us with career and work issues.

Shamanic Counselling

Zack, who recalled the life of an African shaman, had come for a regression because he felt the experience would help him in his counselling work. The memory he accessed revealed that, as many others have found, training in his current work had begun long before this lifetime. Here he describes one of the cases he had to deal with:

> I'm sitting in a round hut. It's quite small. I'm with a woman who is possessed by a bad spirit. Her true self has been split off from her and can't get back in. It's not in charge anymore and an evil spirit is.

I'm calling on the energies of the Earth to help her. They are absorbing the false self that has taken over. Then I'm binding her true self back into her. I don't know how to describe it, but I'm seeing how it happens...

(Later)

That worked out well, but the self that came back was very angry. She wanted to escape from things she had to face, so she wasn't pleased to be back. She caused a lot of problems for me later on.

Afterwards, Zack was able to understand the significance of this particular memory:

Now I know why I'm having difficulties with one of my clients. It's the same sort of thing as that past-life experience. That really helps me to deal with that now. Where I work, we often discuss different methods. I didn't realize it before, but I can see now that I've always been standing up for the shamanic way. That makes so much sense now. I feel that this memory came to give me the confidence of my convictions – and to encourage me to carry on.

The Wise Woman Returns

Kass came for a regression because she was at a personal crossroads in her working life. In response, her inner self gave her the memory of her lifetime as the wise woman of the woodland tribe. It was a happy life – until strangers arrived in the land.

The newcomers were more materially advanced, with colourful clothing and strange possessions. This fascinated most of the tribe and they abandoned the old spiritual ways. It distressed Kass to watch them lose their dignity trading their labour for shiny toys, but she didn't interfere.

All the time that was going on, she and her sisters quietly continued their work providing herbal medicines, communing with the nature spirits and observing the seasonal rituals. Their patience was eventually rewarded. The newcomers left, their toys fell apart and the tribe slowly trickled back to their old way of life.

After the regression Kass talked about what that memory meant to her:

I've recently been offered a promotion at work and it's been worrying me silly. I'm scared in case I don't measure up, even though everyone says that's ridiculous.

But I think I can see now what the real problem has been: it's an old belief that a female shouldn't have authority. That memory made it clear that I once did. And I didn't abuse my power – even when the people ran after things I thought were wrong.

In the end, I think they liked me for that. It was so touching when I was old and dying and they gave me all those lovely gifts and tributes.

I think this came up to show me that I was a leader as a woman once before and I can be again.

It's such a weight off my mind. I feel a lot better about this promotion now. I'm going to tell them tomorrow that I'll accept it.

The Special Message

In Naomi's medicine-woman life she used her powers to try to warn the people of the fort about the danger they were in, provide healing potions and fly in search of her tribe's missing warriors. Towards the end of the regression, she talked about the significance of this memory:

AF: *What are your impressions about this life?*

N: *It was a time of change. Things had been simple and happy for us. We gathered the land to us, like gathering up a child and loving it. Our whole way of life was nurturing.*

We lived simply, but not because we were primitive. We had a lot of subtle knowledge. We drew our wellbeing from the worlds of spirit as well as the Earth. It was part of our natural awareness and we took it for granted.

But our way of life was becoming increasingly threatened. Newcomers from other places were marching in and slowly trampling us and all our ways underfoot.

AF: *Why did this memory come up for you?*

N: *It was to remind me of those values, because we need more of them in the world now. I think I was pretty much the same sort of person then as I am now. Nothing has changed. And that's the message, I think: the same dynamics, the same forces, are still operating. We still need to live that way and hold on to those values. And we still need to be aware of all the dangers and the threats to them.*

I feel as if I'm outside it now and looking at the big picture, where the past and the present are all one thing.

That flying experience was so strong. It really blew me away. I can still feel it. I think it was a real memory, but it was also a metaphor. This whole memory has given me a bird's eye overview, so I can see how those times, and the person I was then, aren't really so different from what's happening now.

Our ancient shamanic wisdom is coming back into the world – but with some important differences. In harmony with the democratic Age of Aquarius, this knowledge is no longer the preserve of a chosen few. Instead of having to call on a shaman, everyone can now use those techniques to access their own inner guidance and healing.

As we learn once more to honour the spirits within all living things, we also honour our own spirits. When we treat the Earth with respect and appreciation, we also respect and appreciate ourselves and one another. These wise old ways will do much to lead us from the wasteland of materialism to the gardens of a happier, more meaningful and ultimately more sustainable world.

YOUR PAST-LIFE SHAMANIC MEMORIES

This visualization will introduce you to your past-life memories in a safe and gentle way. You'll be able to view scenes from your past lives as a detached observer, without needing to relive any of the experiences. Whenever you wish, you can stop the exercise simply by opening your eyes. For extra reassurance, ask your guardian angel or spirit guide to be with you.

Repeat this exercise whenever it feels right. At first you may get only brief glimpses of your memories, but with practice you'll gather a lot of information about your past lives. As you go along, you'll begin to see the bigger picture of your soul's reincarnational journey. This will help you to understand much more about your current life and how it fits into your higher purpose.

◎ *Preparation:* Sit or lie somewhere where you can be quiet and undisturbed.

◎ *Relaxation:* Scrunch up and expand all your muscles, especially your face, hands, arms and shoulders. Then let all your muscles soften and relax.

- *Focus:* Become aware of everything that's underneath you. Sense how comfortable, firm and supportive it is.

- *Centre yourself:* Gaze steadily at a candle or a crystal until you want to close your eyes.

- *Clear your mind:* Breathe slowly and deeply, right down to your stomach. Listen to the sound of your breath.

- *Approach the gateway:* Imagine that you're in a forest clearing. In the centre of this clearing there's a gigantic oak tree. It's so big that you're no taller than the huge roots as they go into the earth.

- *The doorway:* You see a door in the side of the tree. It's big enough for you to go through it. When you feel ready, open the door and enter the giant tree.

- *The stairs:* Inside, you'll see a stairway that spirals deep down into the earth. As you go down those stairs, notice everything that you see or sense around you.

- *Observe and explore:* At the bottom of the stairs, come out of the tree. Find a place that feels comfortable. From there you'll be able to safely observe past-life scenes from times of natural magic unfolding before you. Stay there for as long as you wish.

- *Return:* When you feel that it's time to return, thank all those who have helped you during this exercise. Then come back slowly and gently to your everyday world.

PART II
MAGIC IN RELIGION

*'It was the experience of mystery – even if mixed
with fear – that engendered religion.'*
Albert Einstein

INTRODUCTION

Our soul histories are as haunted by monks, nuns, priests and priestesses as any ancient abbey or temple. Heretics are also there, peeping out from the shadows. These can be quite intense lives and the effects stay with us for long afterwards.

After the joys of the nurturing worlds of natural magic, religious lives may feel like going to school. But while this phase is more mentally focused, it can be just as magical as a shamanic life.

Every religion has its roots in magic – although they all do their best to disown that once they become established and respectable. Good chunks of Indian Vedic literature, the tale of Gilgamesh, the Samavidhana Brahmana and much of Brahmin lore sound just like instructions for sorcery.

Early Christianity used magic openly. The priests did a brisk business in charm-selling, healing, fortune-telling, astrology and exorcism. They smiled upon their followers practising prophetic, psychic and healing powers. Visions and speaking in tongues were not only allowed but encouraged.

As time went by, this encouragement cooled to tolerance. That tolerance later wore thin until it finally disappeared altogether. In 362 the Council of Laodicea forbade the clergy from all paranormal trading except for exorcism. As the Dark Ages deepened, any signs of magical ability among the rank and file became dangerously taboo.

However, the Church managed to hang onto its mystical ceremonies with some deft repackaging. Magic water, spells and rituals were redubbed holy water, miracles and sacraments. This meant that all forms of magic not done by the priests were unholy – so must be the work of the devil. This turned people's natural psychic abilities into a source of guilt and terror.

Even lifetimes later, that unconscious fear still keeps people from unearthing their buried abilities. It also tends to cut people off from the guidance of their own spirit self.

The heavy hand of past-life religion can damage people in other ways too. The power of a religious vow can be so strong that it acts like a spell, trapping a portion of a person's energy in the past. Old commitments to the virtues of poverty and chastity still cast a shadow over many lives, haunting people with abundance and relationship issues.

Formal religion tends to oppress women because they represent the values of the previous phase – intuition, feelings and the powers of the Earth. Being devalued for one's gender leaves its mark on the psyche and may cause a wide range of identity and even gynaecological problems in later lives.

That doesn't mean the men get off scot free. They too can inherit a pervasive sense of unworthiness – one of the biggest blocks to happiness and success in this life.

Religious lives aren't all negative, of course. Many people had beautiful times cloistered away from the wild world, singing and dreaming their way down the mystical path.

They may also have done work to be proud of – feeding the poor, spreading messages of hope, teaching children and tending the sick.

The Church also teaches its acolytes some valuable skills, and learning gained in previous lives is never lost. Even if not consciously recalled, it's easy to pick up old knowledge again and develop it in later lives. Past lives spent pottering in the monastery garden, illuminating manuscripts or conducting the choir may later flower into successful careers in medicine, art or music.

So, although our religious lives may leave us with some wounds to heal, they can also give us significant rewards.

In a vivid dream I once had, I saw a monk working at a manuscript by the light of one candle. Darkness was all around, and a sense of danger. This was many centuries ago, when learning and civilization flickered as feebly as the little candle.

I understood that whatever its faults and shortcomings, in those days the Church was a warm haven for many souls. The message of the dream was clear: although we now condemn much about the medieval Church, it was also a powerful force for good.

Whichever religion we pick, our souls emerge from religious lives with faith in spiritual power, empathy for others and a firm grasp of the importance of social justice, charity, compassion and mercy. These values are like giant non-denominational angels that stride through the world, seeking out ways to make life better for everyone.

Does it make much difference which past-life religion you chose to experience? Probably not. You might have tried more than one of them at different times.

Carl Jung said each person chooses whichever religion suits their stage of development. Of the different religions he said, 'They are only the changing leaves and blossoms on the stem of the eternal tree.'

Past-life awareness makes it easy to heal the wounds of those lives. When we've done that, we are stronger and wiser than we would have been without them.

We can then appreciate the positive gifts of our religious past lives – and look back on them with true peace in our hearts.

9

SOUND EFFECTS

A few years ago one of my regression clients, Barbara, came to Glastonbury with a meditation group. It was on the summer solstice, so they got up well before dawn and went up the Tor to meditate before the sun rose. She told me:

> I'd been to a powerful workshop the day before, so when we went up the Tor I was still in a somewhat altered state of consciousness. Then I think the magic of the Tor did the rest, because I had the best meditation experience ever.
>
> I went back to what I think were Druid times. I became aware of how much knowledge the Druids had. They had much more powerful magic than people think they did. It was nature magic, but not primitive. It was almost scientific.

Barbara had tuned into a time between natural tribal magic and the emergence of a formal priesthood. The shaman was originally doctor, priest, historian, musician and clairvoyant all in one. As time went by, specialists began to take over those functions. For a long time poets, storytellers and musicians kept one foot in shamanic mysticism. Eventually the priests fenced off esoteric knowledge to make it their own special preserve.

But it took a long time for society to become that rigid and compartmentalized. Another of my clients, Blane, regressed to the fluid period before that happened. In this memory, he went back to a time when the bard was also a healer.

The Druid Bard

He recalled being a boy of about seven in a place which felt like England, perhaps around Roman times. He wore a rough tunic with a hood.

Because he showed interest in healing, his family took him to a respected healer who was willing to train students. He became the older man's apprentice, doing chores and learning more every day.

The memory then moved to when Blane had grown into a young adult with long dark hair. He was walking with his staff through a wooded hilly area, heading for a house where he knew he'd be able to stop for the night.

The couple welcomed him with a place by their fire and a bowl of hot stew. They told him their child was ill and asked for his help. He readily agreed and went to look at the little girl.

> She's about six years old. She has long golden hair and is lying on a thick bed of straw with blankets over it. I feel her forehead. It's hot. I ask the family to bring some water and cloths. I put damp cloths around her face and neck. I give her a drink with herbs in it. Then I sing a healing song. The family are just watching very respectfully.
>
> The child falls asleep. The song is working. It's not just a lullaby – there's something else to it that makes it healing in some way.

I feel fairly sure by now that the girl will be alright. We leave her to sleep for the night. The family give me the best bed in the place.

Now it's the next morning. The child is much better. I give them herbs to put in hot drinks for her. I'll stay maybe another day or so to see how it goes, then I'll go back to my tribe.

AF: *What do you do there?*

B: *Healing, and giving them songs. Whenever they go on one of their raids or attacks they like a good song afterwards saying how heroic they all were.*

I heal their wounds with herbs and poultices for the body, and songs for the soul. The soul gets wounded in battle too. In looking back now, I think it was the songs that helped them the most.

(Pause)

I've gone back to a particular memory now. It's night. We're sitting around a big cauldron of stew that's cooking on a fire. The atmosphere is quite sombre. A lot of young men have been killed in a recent battle. Everyone is quiet, just staring into the fire. This is a good time for a gentle song.

I start to sing softly. I can see with my inner eye what I'm singing about – the souls of the dead coming up from the cauldron in the steam. I sing about how they always return to us. This is part of our legends. I can feel the song is comforting the people and giving them heart.

Now I'm watching the scene from high above it. The huge dark land is all around the little camp. The big night surrounds it.

It was a brief experience and yet the memory is so strong – the feeling that for a little while I was able to sing away the sadness and harshness of people's lives.

*I feel so peaceful. That memory was just what I needed. I
don't know how, but I think it's healed me in some way.*

The cauldron is a universal symbol of life, abundance and
regeneration. In the everyday world it represents food and
the safety of community. At deeper levels it stands for the
life-giving power of the womb.

Ancient Celts believed that when warriors died in battle,
they later re-emerged from a magical cauldron. When
they returned they were strong again, but had no memory
and were unable to speak. This was the Celtic version of
reincarnation. It meant that the dead would return to life,
but would be unable to remember or talk about their earlier
lives. Gathered round the fire, gazing at the steam rising
from the cauldron, those who'd lost loved ones in battle
would have been comforted by this.

Sound Power

The healing power of songs was taken for granted in those
days. Recent findings now bear out what those ancient
people knew. In February 2010, the Neurosciences Institute
in San Diego, USA, announced that they had scientifically
proven the healing effects of song. They found that when
we sing, we activate several different areas of the brain at
the same time. This 'rewires' the brain, reconnecting and
reviving areas that have been damaged or shut down – after
a stroke, for example.

Grief, fear or shock can also make us shut down part
of our consciousness as a way of coping. Because songs
reintegrate us, they could be as powerful a way of healing
soul wounds as this past-life memory says they once were.

Ancient civilizations had a sophisticated understanding
of sound that our culture is only now beginning to rediscover.
Archaeologists have found that ancient ceremonial sites such

as Stonehenge and the Pyramid of Kulkulan were designed to create special acoustic effects to enhance religious rituals.

In his regression, Jon described one of those experiences:

> It was in a big enclosed area. There were three priests standing on a high ledge. They wore long white robes and huge head-dresses. Each was in charge of a huge gong, of different sizes. A gigantic one was in the centre.
>
> I was watching them from the ground. There must have been hundreds of us there. The ceremony was a kind of cleansing, blessing and fertility thing all rolled into one.
>
> The priests chanted for a long time. Their voices were really loud. They also made huge bangs on the gongs. The sounds echoed off the walls and went right through us. It felt fantastic.
>
> I think the gongs were there to cleanse us of negative stuff like bad health, and the chanting was to infuse us with positive stuff.
>
> We loved these ceremonies. There were always big parties afterwards. It was a happy time, a happy life.

Ancient Egyptian creation myths say that everything began with sound. 'In the beginning was the word' was originally an Egyptian concept. It meant that everything had its own vibration, which could be translated into a sound.

For the Egyptians, your vibration was your real name. The secret names of the gods were especially important. Because they were the same vibration as the gods, they had great power. This is why Egyptian legend says that when Isis learned the true name of Ra, she was able to cure him of a snake bite.

In ancient Jewish tradition, the secret name of Jehovah could only be said by the high priest on the Day of Atonement

(Yom Kippur). For this ceremony he had to be completely alone in the innermost holy sanctuary, so that no one could ever hear him.

Names of gods and words of power were used more actively in Egyptian religious magic. For ritual use, these could be very long. The true name of one deity was AEOBAPHRENEMOUNOTHILARIKRIPHIAEYEAIPIR KIRALITHONUOMENERPHABOEAI.

A word of power might also be a series of vowels: A EE EEE IIII OOOOO YYYYYY OOOOOOO. Egyptian rituals must have sounded a bit like Tibetan overtone chanting. The purpose of these lengthy chants was so that, like tuning forks, the priests and priestesses would take on the same vibration as the deity's name, and become a direct channel for the god or goddess.

So, for the ancient Egyptians - and countless priests and magicians since then - words were full of magic power. The Egyptians used affirmations in exactly the same way as we do now: to create a desired condition by repeating over and again that it is already so. Perhaps we know how to do this because our ancient Egyptian past-life knowledge is coming back to us now.

During the Christian era, knowledge about the magical power of sound was forbidden to the people and had to go underground. Yet the Church used it extensively in chants, rituals and bell-ringing.

Bells work like gongs - the frequencies go right through our bodies, affecting us at every level. For centuries, church bells were rung not just to call people to prayer but also to dispel the forces of evil and darkness.

Researchers have now found that Gregorian chanting increases energy levels, relieves stress, lowers blood pressure, reduces anxiety and depression and promotes a sense of wellbeing. Beth told me that it had a big effect on her whenever she heard it. It reminded her whole body of the uplifting effects she used to derive from chanting during a past life of religious devotion.

She came for a regression to see if she could recall those times. Although she expected to find the memories of a Christian monk, she went back to a much earlier, unknown civilization:

> I don't know where this is. It feels like a very long time ago. The people look a bit oriental, with light brown skin. Their clothes are colourful. Everything seems very busy and purposeful.
>
> I was ill at that time. I was being carried on a stretcher up some steps into a large building. They put me down in the middle of a huge hallway and just left me there. Nobody came to see about me or anything. Everything was very quiet.
>
> Then this sound started up. It's hard to describe. It built up slowly. There were echoing deep tones booming round and round the hall. I could feel it going through my whole body. It slowly got louder and louder. After a while it was so intense it became almost unbearable. I think I fainted.
>
> The next thing I remember, I was back at home. A woman was giving me something to drink from a bowl. I think she was my mother. I got the impression that I'd been healed by the strong medicine of sound, but I'd have to spend some time recovering from it.
>
> Now I'm being told that this was to remind me of how I first experienced what sound can do. I'm being shown that I had a lot of religious lives after that – mostly Buddhist and Christian. In those lives I always loved the chanting and the bells. That was because I knew deep down, from this earlier experience, just how powerful and magical sound could be.

People once knew how to use sound in all kinds of advanced and specialized ways. For many cultures, it was one of the highest forms of religious magic.

Perhaps these memories are coming up because it's time for us to reclaim that knowledge. As we do, the ancient power of sound may be able to be a positive and healing force in our world once again.

10

MYSTERIES OF
ANCIENT EGYPT

For the ancient Egyptians, sound was just one of a large array of magical tools they had at their disposal. Religion and magic were closely entwined, and central to their lives. In fact they had no word for religion because they didn't see it as separate from everyday life. Their closest word for it was *heka*, which meant activating the *ka*, or inner spirit. *Heka* stood for the god of magic as well as magical power – what we might now call 'the force'.

Perhaps this understanding of the mysteries of life is why, like its vast monuments, ancient Egypt is still the giant of world history. Thriving for over 4,000 years, it's the longest-known civilization on record. In contrast, the Roman Empire ended after 700 years and the British Empire was even shorter.

Because the ancient Egyptian civilization continued for such a long time, it's not surprising that countless people had past lives there. Those memories stand out like stars on the soul journey. They were times when people lived by an ancient wisdom that is now mostly lost.

Yet some traces of that knowledge are still with us. They are usually in disguise, because other cultures incorporated

Egyptian ways and made them their own. For example, the Gnosticism that flourished around 2,000 years ago evolved directly from Egyptian teachings.

If a Bible with footnotes were ever produced, it would be crammed with references to Egypt. Moses' Ten Commandments, as well as the Lord's Prayer, the Sermon on the Mount and other sayings attributed to Jesus, were all lifted directly from ancient Egyptian texts. Even the word 'Amen' is the name of an Egyptian god.

During the Renaissance, the Thoth books of wisdom were rediscovered. They became hugely influential – under the new name of the Hermetic Fragments, after the Greek god Hermes.

Perhaps because of our past lives there, ancient Egyptian attitudes can be traced in many New Age beliefs. The Egyptians thought of the heart as the centre of consciousness. They respected intuition, mysticism and direct inner knowing.

Ma'at was the state of peace, stability and plenty that Egyptian civilization intended as its norm and that it achieved for most of its long history. One of the most important jobs of the priests and priestesses was to maintain the consciousness that created this ambience. By keeping the vibrations high, they created a state of peace and abundance.

Popular myth says that the Egyptians were obsessed with death, but their real focus was actually the non-physical worlds. The *Book of the Dead* is about the journey a spirit can expect to take after leaving the physical body. Egyptians called the other world Amenti, the Kingdom of Osiris, or the 'Good Father's House'. They said it was a place of 'many mansions', or states of consciousness.

Preparing for the next world was one of their most sacred tasks. One of my regression clients, Sandy, recalled a life in ancient Egypt. He was a herbalist then and embalming was also one of his tasks. He saw himself as a devoted servant of the priestess and often went to the temple for higher guidance about his work. The challenge for him in this life was to learn to follow his spiritual path independently, without that supportive framework.

A Special Ritual

Because the priests' role was so central, lives in the Egyptian priesthood could be especially intense. One of Ashton's favourite memories of his priestly past life was the special feast days.

Starting at dawn, a crowd would gather outside the temple. Ashton and his assistants would keep coming out with baskets of ritually prepared petals. They'd scatter the petals over the people like blessings. Ashton said doing this made him feel like a powerful benefactor.

At other times he felt just the opposite. Teaching was one of his duties – and he was troubled because two young girls in his class giggled all the time. They clearly weren't taking his words seriously. So he decided to show them just how powerful the gods could be.

> I've gone to a special hall. It's a very holy place. We stay away to keep it pure. I'm not supposed to be here about a personal matter, but I feel that it's justified.
>
> I'm looking at all the animal head-dresses that are hanging along the walls. The priests wear these only for very special rituals. Wearing them brings the god presence into you. When a priest puts one of these on his head, he's allowing himself to be taken over by its god.

Ashton said he'd worn a head-dress only once before – and had been disappointed because he hadn't felt any holy presence. He explained why they used animal heads to represent the gods:

Very long ago, when the gods came to this land, the people here were like animals. And they worshipped animals. So the gods had to turn themselves into powerful animals in order to teach the people.

They chose their creatures carefully. The special quality of each animal is also the special quality of the god.

When the gods left, they gave us these head-dresses with the promise that whenever we wore them, they would return and work through us.

He nervously did a little dedication, stating that his intention was to increase faith in the gods. He asked to be guided to whichever god – if any – would help him do this.

After a long wait, he nearly gave up. Then he was thrilled to receive an inner message:

It's Horus – the hawk head. I go to that head-dress. I bow before it and do the invocation. I take it down from the wall.

My hands are shaking. I put it over my head. It sits on my shoulders. It's quite heavy. It feels hot and uncomfortable. I do the special breathing to draw in the god presence.

I'm walking down the passage... going to a special room. The two girls are there waiting, standing quietly together – not giggling for a change.

I go to a stone plinth and light some incense. I turn around and start to go through the ritual.

He began to chant to call in the presence of the god. As he did so, he was overjoyed to feel Horus overshadowing him. Allowing his consciousness to recede, he let the god channel through him.

He was aware of something speaking through him to the girls, but didn't know exactly what was said. They later told him Horus had said it was important to respect others because that meant they respected themselves. After that, their whole attitude changed.

The experience also had a major effect on the priest. He realized that what he'd really been struggling with was not the girls' scepticism but his own. They'd been acting as mirrors to his inner doubts. This ritual successfully put all his worries to rest.

Life in a Temple

One of the most important aspects of ancient Egyptian culture was the way it honoured the feminine. Each goddess stood for different aspects of the female psyche and experience. Validated, honoured and protected by the goddesses, Egyptian women had rights and freedoms unequalled by any other culture until the twentieth century.

Zavvi came for a regression at a time when she was slowly extricating herself from a disempowering relationship. A past-life memory came to her like an ally, reminding her of a time when her feminine worth had been strong and secure. The first thing she saw was a girl laughing. She thought she might belong to a group of ladies-in-waiting to a queen. Then she realized this was a temple in ancient Egypt:

I think we're the priestesses. But we don't seem to take it very seriously, so I don't know... I get the impression that we fuss with our hair quite a lot.

We have fun. We do a lot of singing and have a lot of laughs.

I'm looking out of one side of this place. It's open, like a huge veranda with big columns holding it up. We're high up. I can see right out over the countryside.

There's a big thing here that holds water. It's like a font. It's got some sort of handle things on it.

Zavvi then recalled that this was used for scrying. The priestesses looked into it like a crystal ball when people came to them for psychic guidance.

I don't think any special ritual goes with it. It's all done in broad daylight. We just look into the water, see what happens and say what we see. And all the time, the everyday bustle is going on around us. It's all done in a very matter-of-fact way.

AF: *When people come for this do they pay in any way?*

Z: *They just give what they can. That way, people can come who don't have much. They might even do some sweeping or something like that as payment.*

AF: *Does this support the upkeep of the temple?*

Z: *A bit. But we're also centrally maintained. We belong to the whole set-up. We're part of the official religion – the normal priestly function. So although we keep quite distant in a way, we're maintained by the pharaoh. We're part of the fabric of society, but on the very esoteric side.*

AF: *How do you become a priestess?*

Z: *We get picked. The older priestesses go round the villages now and then, just walking around and looking – looking into people's eyes, really.*

That's what happened to me. When I was about six, a tall lady came. She was quite old but very elegant. I was just living in a rough village. I was rather poor, I think. She looked me in the eyes and I looked back at her. Then she put her hand out to me and said, 'This one.'

AF: *How did your parents feel about it?*

Z: *They were happy. Having a child chosen for a temple was a known thing. It was an honour. I mean, I wasn't cut off* *from my parents or anything like that. They came and visited. And I could go and visit them.*

AF: *How does the priestess know which child to pick for the temple?*

Z: *I know this because I learned how to do it when I was older. You can see that they've done this before, in past lives. So we're looking for a kind of recognition. It's actually quite easy to spot. You're looking to see almost – not exactly an old friend, but a six year old's eyes that aren't the eyes of a six year old. There's a depth of wisdom somewhere in there.*

And then you test it. You put your hand out. If they come to you and take it, then they're the right one.

AF: *So you were taken to the temple when you were about six – what then?*

Z: *Well, we used to play a lot. That was nice. Everybody was always very kind. They also taught us things: reading and writing, healing, the holy books – everything we needed to know, really.*

Zavvi described how the priestesses slept in dormitories on narrow beds of rushes and animal furs. Everything was shared, so they had few personal possessions, just their clothes and bits of jewellery. They all ate together in a big refectory.

There's always lovely food: lots of fresh dates, a sort of couscous, a flat bread... some goat meat sometimes. Not too much meat, though. Some vegetables. Sweet pastries flavoured with honey. We like those! Sometimes we have soup. But we don't eat a lot. If they were heavy meals we wouldn't be able to do our work.

AF: *What work is that?*

Z: *Keeping the land stable. Keeping things... in balance.
Correcting imbalances. If there's a lot of bad behaviour
going on, or dissention, or anything unpleasant, it has to be
redressed, otherwise the country will tip into war. What we do
balances it all up so that harmony is restored.*

*We have quite a good reciprocal arrangement with the priests.
They know that they actually get quite a bit of energy from us.
They do most of the outward public stuff, but they come to us
for an awful lot of help and support. They come to get restored
by us.*

*There's constant building going on – big monuments going up
all the time. And a whole priestly thing goes on with it. It's
not a matter of just building something and then afterwards
getting the priests to go and do their bit of blessing on it – it's
not like that at all. They have to go in there constantly. Part
of the building process is the rituals and spells that they plant
into whatever is being built.*

*We also do some of that from time to time. On rare occasions
we go with the priests to the pyramids to do rituals with them
there. That's very powerful, especially when we do our chants.
But we don't do that very often – only when things are at a
critical stage.*

Zavvi recalled how she left that life:

*I'm going up... spiralling up out of my body. There's a very
bright white light. I can see my body lying down there below
me. The other priestesses are standing around it, looking a bit
sad... tidying me up a bit.*

*A few of them are looking up. I think they can see me floating
above them. So I wave my hand... goodbye... and turn... and
skewer off... up... and away...*

The next thing I remember is having a discussion with a few others. The feeling was, Let's evaluate this life now. How did it go? What did you learn? What can you do better next time? – that kind of thing.

There are guides here who help organize your next life – where you're going to go next, what your purpose will be. There's quite a lot of stuff you have to plan. You can't do it on your own, so there are helpers organizing these things.

AF: *What insights did you get about your purpose in that life?*

Z: *It was all about the knowledge I gained in the temple and that kind of empowerment. So that in later times, in future lives, when it would be lost, I would still have some memory of it and I'd be able to remind other people as well.*
After that first big discussion I just wanted to go and have a rest for a bit. And that's fine in this place. I went off and lay down somewhere beautiful, just to assimilate everything.

You don't have to go back into another life right away. The next thing I did was get involved with helping others who'd just left the physical world. I also did a bit of guardian angeling.

AF: *What does that involve?*

Z: *Keeping an eye out for one or two incarnated people. You get assigned to somebody. First you and others help to plan their next life. Then, when they incarnate, you act as their guardian angel – which is nice, because it gives you continuity. And you get to see how difficult it is. We say what we want to do with a life, but when we actually incarnate, it's so hard to remember what we decided.*

I like working from the other side. It's fascinating learning all about how a life gets planned before the next incarnation.

It's also nice being a guardian angel. Trying to remind people – planting little things in their way to remind them of their purpose and help them remember that they're only playing. It's not real. It really is very hard for people to remember.

AF: What would you do if the person went badly off track in some way?

Z: *Sometimes you have to do some quite serious rescue jobs. You can't interfere with free will, of course, but you can plant things. You can put things in their way to nudge them, to remind them. But whether or not they notice is up to them.*

We also try to communicate with them. Dreams are the best way, or when they're daydreaming, or meditating. If they go out for a walk, sometimes you can get in then.

It's all faded now. I think that's all I'm going to get today.

Afterwards Zavvi said the main impression that memory made on her was how happy she and the other girls had been as priestesses:

You always think ancient temples and places like that must have been full of sombreness, and we were in touch with some quite deep things, but we did it all so happily. We knew it was important to keep our hearts light. Maybe that was the only way we could have done what we did.

I like that attitude. I think we could do with a bit more of it today. It doesn't mean not believing in the things we value, it's just a matter of doing it all with a lighter heart. These memories have been a great reminder to me of how important joy is on the spiritual path.

11

GLASTONBURY ABBEY: THE HIDDEN SIDE

Because I live in Glastonbury, a lot of people come for regressions about their past lives here. One of the richest sources of these memories is the abbey.

Glastonbury Abbey was famous for being the first Christian church in the land. According to legend, it was founded by Joseph of Arimathea himself. In its medieval heyday, it was the wealthiest monastery in England. It was a leading spiritual and educational centre - like Eton and Canterbury cathedral rolled into one.

The monks gave the abbey's standing a big boost in 1191 when they announced that they'd found the remains of King Arthur and Queen Guinevere buried in the grounds. Tourists and pilgrims flocked to Glastonbury for hundreds of years after that, creating a golden era of popularity and prosperity for the abbey.

It must have meant a lot to be part of this prestigious place. This may be why some of the monks still linger here in one form or another. Over the years many people have reported seeing the ghosts of monks wafting around Glastonbury.

Between 1907 and 1922 the architect and church restorer Frederick Bligh Bond learned to communicate with some of those monks through automatic writing. They helped him with his researches, telling him where to dig for the original structures of the abbey, as well as where some rare blue glass was buried. Later excavations showed that all these communications had been correct. This infuriated the Church authorities and they immediately sacked Bond. His account of the whole experience is in his book *Gate of Remembrance*.

One of the spirit monks he contacted enjoyed reminiscing about his past life at the abbey:

> *I loved the rain on our hundred roofs and myriad voices that came from the waterspouts, when the gargoyles shouted each to each, and the cloisters whispered comfort and refreshment as we lay under the dormer roofe in parched and sultry nights. I didde sleepe on the south side, hard by the great gabell, and soe I heard the sound whilst the others slept. Vai Mubi, that it is departed and the voices are heard no more.*

Monks wistful for the abbey in its heyday also return here as physically reincarnated people. When Diara came to Glastonbury she unearthed not only her past life in the abbey, but some of its darker secrets as well.

'Even before getting to the abbey, I had a dream about it,' she told me. 'I was standing in a corner by a stone wall and said, "There are buried treasures here." That was the whole dream. But it was so vivid.'

In her regression, Diara went back to a time soon after the abbey had been shut down by Henry VIII as part of his countrywide Dissolution of the Monasteries. He did this partly to destroy the power base of the Pope in England

and Wales and partly to grab the lands and wealth of the monasteries for himself.

By then, Glastonbury Abbey had become one of the richest in the country and the king was determined to seize its assets. Abbot Richard Whiting resisted the takeover for as long as he could. Many think he used that brief time to smuggle out much of the abbey's treasures. For doing this, the king had him hung, drawn and quartered on Glastonbury Tor. Some say his ghost still haunts the old funerary procession route of Dod (i.e. 'dead') Lane in Glastonbury.

Tales are still told about where that missing treasure might have gone. Many of the rumours say that it was taken through an underground tunnel to hidden caves within the Tor.

These events would have been fresh in the mind of Diara's past self as a recent abbey monk. She recalled walking sadly round the grounds, noticing how quickly the abbey was falling apart. While there, her past self met an old friend – another ex-monk:

> *We embrace and walk on in silence. We don't have to say anything. We both know why we're here.*
>
> *Dusk is falling. It's not safe here after dark these days. We head back into town. My friend says he's on his way to meet someone who can help us.*
>
> *We go to a tavern. There are lit candles on some of the tables. We've got grey tankards of some drink. I think it's a kind of beer.*
>
> *I feel uneasy. This place is full of shady characters. My friend is talking quietly with the man he came to meet. He looks like a gypsy...*
>
> *Now we're back in the abbey. It's late at night. I'm still with those two. A couple more gypsies have joined us. One of them*

is a woman. She looks half wild. I'm afraid of her. She might
be a witch.

My friend gives the gypsies something that I recognize. It's one
of the old treasures from the abbey – a jewelled cross. He must
have stolen it before he left. A lot of that went on. We felt
justified. The abbot turned a blind eye to it.

The gypsies are doing some sort of black magic with this
treasure. My friend and I are standing to the side, just
watching. They're chanting words in a language I don't know.
They make passes over the object with their hands held in
odd positions. They're raising it higher and higher, almost
screaming the words.

Now they suddenly crouch down to the ground. I think they're
burying the cross. Then they do things over that spot, chanting
all the time. I can see their eyes sometimes and it's frightening.
They look possessed. I cross myself and say a prayer.

We're walking away from there now. They tell me this spell
will bring misfortune to the king for what he did here and will
protect the abbey from any more evil. That makes me feel a
bit better about it.

Now I'm being shown some of the other things that went on
at that time. When the monasteries were shut down, a lot of
magical workings were done against the king. Not just here –
all over the country.

Many ex-monks used their knowledge about things like
healing and herbs to make ends meet. A few of them joined
forces with gypsies and witches and started doing black magic
with them.

I'm also being shown what the higher-ranking monks did – the
abbots and so on. Some of them knew big secrets – heretical
stuff, things the Church didn't want anyone to find out.

*After the monasteries were closed down, the senior monks
started talking about these things. It all started to leak out
– but very quietly, because it was so dangerous. Some of the
monks got involved with secret societies. I think they may even
have started some.*

Afterwards Diara said the gypsy spell was cast very close to
the spot she was shown in her dream.

'But I don't think that cross is there anymore,' she said.
'The buried treasure the dream referred to was more to do
with remembering the life I had there. I have a feeling that in
another life I got involved with one of those secret societies.
So that's the next thing for me to explore.'

Memories in Stone

Another voice from that time came from Wendy's abbey
experience. It was the first time she'd been to Glastonbury.
She went into the abbey and settled into a quiet sunlit
corner to soak up the atmosphere. As she sat there, a door
to the past suddenly opened in her mind and a cupboardful
of images, impressions and feelings all tumbled out at once.
It was so muddled that she came for a regression to make
sense of it. This is what she discovered:

*I'm sitting at a large table. It's quite a wealthy-looking
room. I'm a churchman, Catholic, quite high up – and
I'm extremely worried. We've been warned that the king is
planning to shut us all down.*

AF: *Who warned you?*

W: *We have contacts at court who tell us things. It was no
surprise. We've been discussing this possibility for a long time.
Great danger is coming for all Catholics in this country,
especially the good, simple folk. People like me can do things*

to safeguard our interests – on the material level, anyway. On the spiritual level, I have some difficult adjustments to make. The Church was a refuge for me. I know it had its flaws, but it was my world. So I feel lost. And desolate.

(The memory moved forward to the next development.)

The king went ahead: he shut us all down. Those were terrible years. But all that was over long ago. I'm in the ruins now – what's left of our beloved Glastonbury Abbey. I'm sitting on a pile of stones. This place has fallen apart, but it's letting the sunlight in. I shut my eyes and feel the warm sun on my face and on the back of my hands. It's like a balm to my soul. It's healing my sadness about what happened.

(Pause)

Touching the stones is taking me even further back now, to other stones, long ago, the stones of another faith.

I've gone to a place that looks like Avebury. There's a stone circle. It's dark, but dawn is breaking. People are coming. I can hear their chanting.

Now I can see them in the distance. It frightens me. I know that the one leading the procession was me in a past life. I don't want to watch, but I have to.

AF: Why don't you want to watch?

W: I think I did terrible things. He's begun now: it's a seasonal ritual to bless the land and the people.

I love their chanting. I'd forgotten how beautiful it was. It's good to hear this part of it again.

Oh dear. Now it's time for the sacrifice. Oh... it's just a small creature. What a relief.

AF: Why is there a sacrifice?

W: *They believe it will bring them protection from the gods. It has great meaning for them. They feel safer and stronger for it.*

There, now he's showing his bloody hands to the people. They're all putting up their hands to receive the power of the sacrificial blood. He believes in what he's doing. He means to work good for the people and the land.

We were honouring the old Earth magic. There really is magic in the Earth. There are many things we knew then that people today don't understand.

Over a cup of herbal tea afterwards, Wendy shared these insights:

My old Catholic churchman recovered from the shock of the Dissolution. The turning-point was that day in the abbey when he saw the sun coming through the broken walls. He saw it as a message from God saying that in a deep way everything was alright.

When I went to the abbey the other day – I think it was the first time I've been back there since then – I had no thoughts about past lives, but I sat down in the sun and shut my eyes exactly as I had on that day. I suppose that's what triggered the jumble of memories.

I didn't expect to go back to stone circle stuff, but I'm glad I did. I've always had a feeling that I abused occult powers in the past. When I saw that procession, I was sure this was it: I was about to see how evil I'd been. But it was fine. I saw there was nothing bad about it.

While I was watching that, I realized that my guilt about it had come from that Catholic life. Now, it's as though there's a weight off my mind that I didn't even know was there.

Psychometry is the art of being able to touch or hold an object and sense its past history. Psychometrists say that stone is the best carrier of information. The ceremonial stone markers of sacred sites must be full of memories, especially for those who had past-life experiences there.

Glastonbury Abbey was built on an older religious centre, so some of its stones would have come from that more ancient site. Perhaps this is why touching them helped Wendy to recall not only her abbey life but also an earlier pagan life.

After the Dissolution of the Monasteries, local people took the abbey's stones to use in their own buildings. It was partly a way of keeping some of that magic for themselves. Many an old home around Glastonbury still has these special stones in places of honour as lintels, doorsteps or hearthstones. Psychics who tune in to them say they have great stores of tales to tell.

Even without touching the stones, visiting an old religious site is one of the best ways to revive past-life memories from that place. Pilgrimages to the ancient temples of Mexico and South America are well known for sparking off surprising images, realizations – and sometimes even more.

A friend who went on a spiritual tour of ancient Mayan sites said that one of their exercises took place in a temple of fertility. In a special ceremony there, while caressing an ancient stone fertility symbol, they each asked the old gods for whatever abundance they wished to multiply in their lives. Soon after that tour, one of the women was overjoyed to find she was pregnant – years after she'd lost hope of that ever happening.

For most of us, it's magic enough just to become aware of our past selves from those places – and, like Wendy, realize that they are not to be feared after all.

❖ ❖ ❖

12

FORBIDDEN KNOWLEDGE

Forbidding something is one of the surest ways to make it attractive. Anything that's taboo develops an aura of glamour that many find hard to resist. Whatever religion declares to be heretical automatically becomes a magnet for the curious.

The danger of forbidden knowledge gives it extra significance which almost guarantees that people will pursue it. Past lives on this path are among our most adventurous, drawing us into dramas that may span more than one lifetime.

The Persian Tutor

Pam recalled a past life in a country that she said felt like Persia, many centuries ago. She was a high-born young girl living in a palatial home. Girls weren't usually educated in that world, but because she was lively and intelligent, her father hired the best tutors he could find to instruct her.

When she reached her early teens, one of her tutors saw her potential and began to teach her secret knowledge:

He was quite old – well, that's how I saw him anyway. He always wore a turban and a long robe and sandals.

We used to work in a room that was high up in a tower. It overlooked a courtyard with a fountain in it. I'd look at the people down below and think how amazed they'd be if they knew what I was learning up there.

There was definitely a sense that this knowledge could give powers to anyone who had it. It felt scientific and magical at the same time. I loved learning these things. And I really did keep quiet about it. I didn't breathe a word to anyone.

But then one day my tutor suddenly disappeared. All my lessons were stopped. Nobody told me why and I was afraid to ask. Soon after that I was married off.

As time went by, she became wrapped up in her family and children. But she never forgot her tutor, or the things he'd tried to teach her. His disappearance left her with a sense of something missing and unfulfilled. It created a yearning that remained with her beyond that lifetime:

That life started me on a quest. In lifetimes since then I've always been seeking out hidden knowledge – the things we aren't supposed to know. I think it's my long-term mission. I still don't feel that I've found what I'm looking for. But I'm sure that one day I will.

Guarding the Spirit

The path to secret knowledge can take on many different guises – sometimes it's like a quiet country lane, other times more like a fast highway. In one life we may pursue our purpose alone, in another as part of a group.

Larry went back to a life within a heretical sect in fifteenth-century Spain. He recalled one of their most secret rituals:

I'm in a place with blue and white geometric patterns on the floor. Two men and two women are here. We're doing some sort of ritual. I've got a metallic device strapped on my hand. It's black, silver and gold. I'm also holding a kind of wand. It has two prongs.

We're preparing a gateway for the soul, for the spirit of someone who has just passed away. We help to direct its journey through a special gateway that we have created on the esoteric level. This takes the spirit in a safe, protected way to where it can reunite with the others.

We do this because we're heretics. We have to keep ourselves hidden from the authorities and be careful all the time. This is why we keep the departing spirit safe and hide it from detection – because certain others may see the soul leaving and interfere with its journey.

It's much more difficult to conceal things on the esoteric plane. The spirit that has just left the body is a bit disorientated. If it's seen by others at this sensitive stage, it may inadvertently give away secrets about us. So we direct the soul through a special tunnel where it can't be seen by others. We also create esoteric barriers around this ritual.

Some spirits find their way swiftly and easily. Others get lost and need a bit of gentle nudging. That's what this wand is for: it's an energy director. The device on my hand transmits energy from me to the wand.

AF: *What else does your group do?*

L: *We train children to become psychics and to become a form of missionary. We also do loyalty tests. There's always danger from the lack of discretion of others. So we test them by telling them secrets that aren't real secrets. Then we see if they keep them.*

Some years later, they heard that the Inquisition had found out about them and was coming to get them. They fled to the hills outside Valencia, where Larry eventually froze to death.

Even though this regression took place on a hot summer day, at that memory he began to shiver and pull a blanket up around himself. Once he'd gone past that point, he pushed the blanket off again.

Enjoying a cold fruit juice afterwards, he discussed the insights he'd received:

> It's to do with religion. I think I've had a love–hate relationship with it for many lifetimes, sometimes fighting it – that never seemed to get me anywhere – sometimes accepting it – that never seemed to last. Maybe it's time for a new approach.

He also realized that it took more than one lifetime to complete a mission. He said that gave him a wonderful feeling of relief – perhaps because he'd been unconsciously pressuring himself to 'do it all' in this lifetime:

> When I look at the world, I always see more bad than good. For as long as I can remember, I've felt as if it's up to me to do something about it – and as quickly as possible. When that life ended, my first feeling was how futile it had all been. But in the afterlife world, a spirit guide showed me another way to see it. This memory has reminded me of what he said: that it's better to take a more philosophical, long-term view of our spiritual missions – and to know that good will win in the end.

The Meek Monk

Sometimes our soul's quest for secret knowledge takes us to lives when we become deeply immersed in the institutions that we want to investigate. The image of humble monks scratching away with their quill pens by candlelight may not always be what it seems.

Paula came for a regression because she wanted to shed light on some disempowerment problems in her life. She often felt put-upon and found it hard to stand up for herself. The following memory revealed how that had begun - and much more as well.

Paula went back to the life of a scholarly monk whose job was to copy manuscripts. He knew much more Latin than he ever admitted to anyone at the monastery. Without those in charge realizing it, he was able to translate and understand many of their secret documents:

> I've been learning how the Church really works. I've been slowly piecing together the reality – the truth – behind the dogma. There are a lot of things that contradict what the Church says is true. A lot. They only allow one story to be told and everything else is heresy. But this heresy is the true history.

AF: *Can you remember any of the true history?*

P: *Some things – very strange things. They're hard for me to understand. There were women apostles. They were as important as the male apostles. Some of the miracles were old Egyptian magic. Some of them were things done by other magicians, much later – miracles that were nothing to do with Jesus. All that has been very shocking to me.*

Aware of the danger, he kept quiet about these discoveries. Wanting to find out more, he adopted a docile manner to keep the forbidden documents coming his way. This went on for years.

We moved to a discussion with Paula's spirit guides about this memory. They explained how she still behaved as if she was in that situation. This was the source of her disempowerment – the belief that if she doesn't appear to be submissive, she'll be in grave danger.

> They're showing me other lives around the theme of religious repression, especially of sexuality. They say that was more of a factor in the monk's life than I realized. They're explaining how suppression of sexuality is the key to suppressing the whole person.

> Now they've taken me to another life I had that was involved with similar things. I'm a priest this time. I'm in a hayloft, reading manuscripts in secret. I have to provide official investigators with religious documents. I'm not sure if it's the Inquisition or not. But before I do that, I edit them up there in the hayloft. I know that some of this information will be dangerous for them to find. These investigators are determined to destroy teachings that don't meet with their view of the world. So I'm cutting those bits out.

AF: What bits are you taking out?

P: Stuff about the relationship between sexuality and spirituality. And things to do with women. I have another book here – this is very secret. They must never find this one. It has no writing on its pages. I think it's invisible ink for secrecy. I'm very afraid. If they find some of the things that are in this book, I'll be tortured and killed.

AF: What sort of things are they?

P: It's to do with the secret teachings of women. It's partly about teaching women things that have been forbidden to them, but it's also about women who were spiritual leaders – with some very interesting things to say.

> I'm tearing out the pages and ripping them up. I feel a lot of sadness about doing this, but I'm determined that it won't

get into the hands of the Church. Because I know that one of their secret purposes is to collect all the esoteric knowledge they can get their hands on. They're doing this to keep it from the people, to keep them ignorant and to use it for their own ends.

I thought I could keep this book hidden. But I know they are coming. Maybe not today, but soon. They suspect that I have something like this.

I'm taking all the bits of paper downstairs now. With a very heavy heart, I throw them on the fire. I sit and watch as all the little pieces burn up.

I've started to see fleeting glimpses in the fire of other past lives. There was a time when I was much more involved with occult matters. I think it was some sort of alchemy. But something went wrong. I got my fingers burned in more than one way.

That life fades... now I'm seeing glimpses of sex magic in the temples of ancient Egypt – colourful, powerful ceremonies. I think they were trying to draw some kind of higher power into the temple.

The curtain falls on that... now I'm being shown that there was some sort of occult side to the Black Death. Something very strange was going on at that time. I'm seeing a rather macabre symbol about it. I see hundreds of people dying of the plague. Their skeletons go into the earth. But later the skeletons come back up again from the earth and point at certain people. I can't see who they are... and it's all fading now.

A few weeks later I asked Paula if I could borrow her regression tape again to check something on the transcript. I was rather surprised when she told me she'd thrown it into a lake.

She said she'd suddenly been overwhelmed by the feeling that it contained dangerous knowledge that might fall into the wrong hands. It was an uncanny echo of the time she'd burned her secret books before the Inquisition could find them.

As it turned out, though, this odd action was a blessing in disguise, as it made her realize just how powerfully that fear had been clutching her heart all this time. After that, she was finally able to release its hold over her.

Many of us have led lives similar to Paula's, when we had to keep quiet about things that were dangerously taboo. The intensity of that fear can ingrain those ways deeply into our souls, so that we continue creating similar dramas lifetimes after the original situation has passed. But as we become aware of the source of these fears, they lose their power over us. In the process we not only heal ourselves but may also discover some strange treasures in the hidden passages of history...

13

ORIENTAL WAYS

I n the long history of our soul journey, we experience many different kinds of religion. As we do this, our inner self can pick the best from all of them to formulate our long-term foundation beliefs.

We also engage with certain religions to develop particular aspects of ourselves. That includes lives of heresy or dissent. These experiences may be strengthening, but can also be traumatic. After going through them, we may choose to recover and heal with a more soothing life in a completely different religion.

One summer morning I had an excited telephone call from Alexa, an old friend I hadn't seen for a while. She'd just returned from a trip to Japan and had so much to tell me, we decided to meet for coffee at one of Glastonbury's garden cafés.

The first thing she said was: 'I now know for sure that I had a past life in Japan!'

This realization had been triggered by her visit to a Shinto shrine. She said it had felt like coming home:

> They give the tourists little instruction leaflets on the
> customs to observe while there. I took one look at it and
> almost threw it away – it was all so obvious. I knew
> exactly what to do, every step of the way. I was so happy
> to be there, I was even crying a bit at one point.

Before this experience, she'd picked up a few clues about her oriental past lives from dreams, synchronicities and her reactions to certain films:

> I've seen two films about the lives of geishas. They both
> hit me really hard. It felt so real – as if my own memories
> had come to life. I've had some striking dreams about that
> as well.

Alexa later dug up those dreams and e-mailed them to me. She'd never been to the East before and knew no one from there, and yet she'd had many dreams about oriental-looking people.

In one of them, she was practising using a large fan in a formal ceremonial way. She felt it was part of her training to be a geisha.

'I think this is why I feel comfortable with all the niceties of formal etiquette,' she said. 'People with bad manners really annoy me.'

Another dream was especially dramatic:

> I was in a high-class Japanese 'tea house' kind of place. I
> worked there as a hostess – a geisha.

> One day I was in the garden, looking at the pretty fish in
> the pond. Someone came and warned me that a certain
> man had arrived. I was really afraid of him. I knew he
> was interested in me, but he was very dangerous.

*It was strictly against the rules, and a big risk to take,
but I went and hid behind the tall baskets in the laundry
room so that I wouldn't have to entertain him at the tea
ceremony.*

*Our house attracted wealthy and powerful people. A
lot of intrigue went on there. This man was part of a
group that used black magic. They were called something
strange – 'the cats that ride the crabs'. I don't know what
that means.*

*If that man decided to become my patron, I wouldn't
have any choice about it – I'd have to go with him and
leave the tea house. That would mean joining his black
magic group. And no one who got mixed up with them
ever got away. If they tried, they ended up dead, because
they knew too many secrets. That was why I was so afraid
of him.*

Alexa later came to explore these memories a bit more
through regression. It turned out that she had managed
to escape the attentions of the man she feared. She was
convinced that was because she'd gone to a nearby shrine
every day to pray to the spirits for protection.

Her gratitude for this deliverance turned her into a
devotee. In her next life, she became a holy dancer at one
of the big Shinto temples. Her formal geisha dance training
had prepared her well for that:

*Temple dancing wasn't done for entertainment, it was
primarily for the spirits. We danced to honour them,
keep in touch with them and draw their power into the
temple. When I danced I sometimes used to see signs of
their presence.*

*It was such a wonderful, magical life. That's why I felt
as though I'd come home when I visited the shrines in
Japan. I don't know if a westerner can, but I'd love to
take up Shintoism.*

The word *Shinto* means 'the way of the gods'. It's the original
folk religion of Japan, a bit like early Celtic magic in Britain.
Both ways believe that *kami*, or spirits, are everywhere and
inhabit all natural things. In the Shinto tradition, people
pray and make offerings to the spirits at special shrines,
which can be in the home or more public places.

After Buddhism spread to Japan around the sixth century,
hostilities flared up every now and then between the old
and new ways. But those differences were soon settled.
Buddhism never demonized or persecuted Shintoism in the
way Christianity did paganism. Shinto magic and Buddhist
philosophy now co-exist in harmony, with many people
happily belonging to both systems at the same time.

Alexa found that she'd taken those Japanese lives as
an antidote to more troubled lives in medieval Europe,
when she had to hide her magical knowledge to preserve
her life. After that experience, she needed a breather from
persecution. Her Shinto lives provided a safe haven where
her spirit could blossom again.

Through most of Asia, magic and religion are
inseparably entwined. Chinese belief in magic is older than
recorded history and the Chinese have a vast number of
books on the subject. Sorcerers – who could be male or
female – enjoyed a high status and played important roles
in court and public life.

While Chinese Taoism has a philosophical base, it's also
at ease with the magical arts of *feng shui*, astrology, *tai chi*,
herbalism and *qi gong*. However, the more esoteric aspects
of *qi gong* still hover on the outer borders of mainstream

acceptance. For many years it had to stay completely secret because it trained people to tap directly into the magical power of the *chi*. My *qi gong* teacher from Beijing told us it was so forbidden in the old days they had to practice at 3 a.m. to make sure no one would see them.

In one of his classes, I remember a young woman being deeply affected when the exercises took her back to a Chinese past life. She talked about her memories of doing this form of movement meditation on a hill outside her house. It was in an isolated area, and she had a panoramic view of the countryside. Doing the exercises in class again brought back all the feelings of spiritual flowering that she'd enjoyed in that life.

Of course, India is the famous home of magical religion in all its myriad forms. This can be traced directly to the profound influence of the Vedas. At over 3,000 years old, these Sanskrit writings are the most ancient texts in the world. Indian tradition says that higher powers revealed the Vedas directly to the *rishis*, or seers.

There are four books: the *Rig, Sama, Yajur* and *Atharva* Vedas. The *Atharva* Veda is the magical one. It's full of mantras, rituals, incantations, spells and charms. The word *mantric* in India means 'magician' – someone who knows how to use mantras for magical workings.

The Vedas, Upanishads and *Bhagavad Gita* are the great roots that nourish the spirituality of India. The big key these books provide is the knowledge that spiritual attainment is available to everyone. Magical powers, or *siddhis*, are the result of personal evolution and not an evil to be suppressed.

Brahmins are the traditional priest caste of India and also some neighbouring countries. They're in charge of all religious ceremonies, from pre-birth to after death. Their rituals are primarily magical and it's rumoured that they have secret books of magic to draw on.

One of my friends has a Brahmin spirit guide who sometimes appears to her in meditation. He once told her that she was a Brahmin in a former life, when she knew how to use religious magic in many powerful ways. He's helping her to gradually integrate her old knowledge in ways which support her as she is now.

Whether Brahmin or not, there are people in India with paranormal powers such as levitation, shapeshifting, bi-location, taming wild animals, divination, walking on water, telepathy, curing physical problems, travelling huge distances very quickly, materializing objects, invisibility, the spontaneous emanation of perfumes, changing the weather and appearing to their devotees in the astral body or dreams. Tales of Indian miracles and mysteries would fill at least another book, if not an entire bookshelf. They show us the extraordinary possibilities that are latent within everyone.

They also make it clear that the physical world is not what it seems. In Madras in 1801 Sir Thomas Munro, later British Governor there, had a startling experience. He was faced with the apparition of Raghavendra Swami, who had passed on about 200 years earlier. The *swami* advised the official to avoid a suspicious financial arrangement. Sir Thomas took the advice and never regretted it. Along the way, he also revised all his ideas about the nature of reality.

One evening I went to a metaphysical talk in the upper room of the historic George and Pilgrim hotel in Glastonbury. During the interval, a friend introduced me to Kayla. She told me that she was in touch with a past self from India who had become a kind of guide in her life. There wasn't time to go into it then, and she was going home to London the next day, but she said she'd e-mail me about it. Here is what she sent:

It all started because I desperately needed some inner peace. A lot of stressful things had happened in my life. I was in such a negative state I felt that I was spiralling downward in a really bad way. I tried to meditate, but I couldn't. One day I screamed out from my heart, 'Somebody please, please, please help me!'

That night I had an amazing dream. I knocked on the door of a beautiful house. It was on a hill, with wonderful views and cool breezes. I just knew this was in India.

The door opened. The man who lived there was standing in front of me. There was a huge feeling of recognition, as if we'd always been close, like brother and sister. It was such a joy to meet again.

I went inside with him. I somehow knew without being told that he'd devoted his life to studying the great spiritual books. He'd also learned a lot from various gurus at different times. He took my hands in his and our hands melted together. We were both smiling the same smile. That was the end of the dream.

When I woke up I knew that man was a past self of mine. The next time I tried to meditate, I went to that house. It made meditation easy. I'd just go and sit in one of my favourite places. I didn't always see anyone else there, but whenever I went there I found a bit more inner peace. Little by little I began to feel better and my life started to calm down.

Then in my meditations I began to see this man more often. We started to have chats. I'd tell him my problems and he'd give me good advice. He's helped me through so much now. Sometimes he asks my advice as well. He loves hearing about all the New Age developments that are happening nowadays.

*I know this might all sound a bit weird, but it's
completely real to me. And it lifted me out of such a
bad hole. It really is one of the best things that has ever
happened to me.*

Our former incarnations aren't dead and gone – they're a living part of our greater self. Like a family, we can be there to help and support one another. Past lives of religious magic can be especially strong allies. With all the knowledge we gained in those times, they are an important part of our souls.

In some ways, these wise past selves may almost seem like spirit guides. When we realize they are really us, it becomes easy to reclaim our true selves: multi-dimensional spiritual beings, on a long and fascinating journey of discovery.

14

SPELLBOUND

B ehind its solemn mask, formal religion is actually a potent force of magic. It uses the same tools that magicians do: rituals, chants, names of power, symbols, talismans – and vows.

Religious vows are especially powerful. Mighty ceremonies seal them in, imprinting the subconscious deeply enough for those vows to cast a spell on us that can last well beyond that lifetime.

These vows are usually appropriate and welcome at the time. On the long trail of the spiritual journey, religious and monastic lives are often a good choice. They can benefit us in so many ways. But once we've moved on from those lives, the intensity of those old vows can sometimes hold us back. An earlier commitment to poverty, chastity and general self-denial may then continue to haunt us. Like invisible hands, these old vows reach out from the past and cast shadows on our attempts to live in joyful abundance or have meaningful relationships.

When something is unconscious it has power over us, but once we become conscious of it, it loses that power.

REMOVING THE RESTRICTIONS OF OLD VOWS

If you think your life might have been restricted by an old religious vow, this alone is a positive development. It means you can now dissolve that spell and remove its negative effects from your life. Here are five simple and effective ways to do this:

◎ It's always helpful to access the past life when a problem began. Simply knowing how an issue started is the golden key to release you from it. Ask your inner self for this information and then trust what comes up. The answers you seek will come to you in meditations, dreams, synchronicities or sudden realizations.

◎ Use your logic to rethink the whole matter. Write down all the reasons you no longer take the old viewpoint about the issue – abundance, for example – and what you now think about it.

◎ Create a simple affirmation, for example: 'As I follow my spiritual path I am blessed with love, abundance and happiness.' Write it out in big colourful letters and put it where you'll see it every day. Repeat it to yourself as often as possible.

◎ Work with it at symbolic levels. Imagine a symbol of the old limiting vow or belief – perhaps as a broken old shoe or a binding chain. Watch this image crumble into dust and a fresh breeze then scattering it all away. In its place, see a beautiful flower blossoming – the symbol of your positive new understanding.

◎ Physical therapies can also be hugely effective. Our bodies hold key past-life effects at cellular level. Once you've reworked a memory, vow or belief that no longer serves your growth, an aromatherapy massage may be all you need to remove the last traces of it.

The Grecian Priestess

Chastity vows often lie dormant until the person takes up a spiritual path. Then the old belief that spirituality means purity may wake up and swing into action.

Alyson's marriage broke up soon after she began to follow her deeper mission. She also started to gain weight which she found very difficult to shift.

During her regression she went back to a life as a temple priestess in ancient Greece. At that time she'd fervently believed that a truly spiritual path had to be a celibate one. In the latter part of that life she had become a senior priestess in the temple. By then, liberal new ways were coming in. The younger priestesses placed little of the old value on their virginity. Alyson's last days there were filled with anger about this.

In the second part of the session she went to a gazebo of light in a beautiful garden. There she met her guardian angel, a tall shining figure in white robes. He told her that one of the reasons her marriage had broken up was because when she'd found her spiritual path, her old belief about the need for celibacy had kicked in.

This wasn't a complete mistake, however. She and her ex-partner had always been destined to follow different paths. A parting of the ways was inevitable sooner or later. In her heart she'd known this all the time.

The weight gain was an unconscious way of keeping potential new partners away from her. Understanding that, she could now make a more conscious choice about the whole issue.

Alyson's guide assured her that she didn't have to stay single because of following a spiritual path. If she wished, a more like-minded partner could come into her life at some time.

Afterwards Alyson said she felt as if a huge burden had been lifted from her. The next time I heard from her, she'd lost the extra weight but wasn't too bothered about getting another partner. She was just happy to be following her inner mission with a new sense of freedom.

Positive Vows

Not every solemn vow we make has a bad effect on us. We also take vows that have positive effects and guide us on our soul journey for many lifetimes.

In a way, all our heartfelt decisions are like religious vows that we make to ourselves. Our biggest decisions take up residence in the psyche to ensure that they will be fulfilled. It doesn't matter if we consciously forget about them – they keep on working, invisibly guiding our actions and decisions. This can go on for lifetimes until we've fulfilled our inner promise to ourselves.

When lovers, friends or families are pulled apart, it's the most natural thing to vow to find each other and be together again one day. When we do meet our loves again – maybe lifetimes later – there's an instant sense of recognition. Many people have had this experience. You can't explain it, but in your heart you know that someone you've just met is an old friend in some way.

When Pam lost her tutor in her Persian life, she was helpless to do anything about it at the time, so she did the only thing she could do: she vowed to herself that she'd somehow continue her studies for his sake. And one day she would find him again.

'I think that's been driving me ever since,' she said. 'I couldn't do much about it for the rest of that life. But in my lives after that, I always made sure that I'd incarnate into a situation where I could carry on seeking out that knowledge. I don't think I've found him again yet. But I'm sure I will one day.'

Sometimes we make vows to one another in the between-life worlds before coming back here. This is why some people are always there for you and you for them. These strong invisible connections between us are one of the things that make life magical.

Another positive vow we can make is when we swear to repay a good deed. Even if we don't do it in that lifetime, a chance will come in another life. This is why people sometimes pop up out of the blue and help out in surprising ways.

A Friend Returns

On holiday in the West Country, Suzanne lost a shoe – but found an old friend from long ago.

> It was after dark and I was walking along a rough country road. There were no street lights of course and I didn't have a torch. It had been raining and was very muddy.
>
> Then I suddenly stepped into a deep pothole – right up to my knees. At first I was just annoyed. But when I tried to get out of it, I found I was stuck. I could feel myself sinking. I panicked and started screaming for help.
>
> After what felt like ages, I heard a man's voice calling back to me from over the field. What a relief that was! It was quite a struggle, but he eventually got me out of that hole. I left one shoe behind, but I didn't care by then.
>
> He was so kind. He took me to his farmhouse nearby and gave me a strong cup of tea. Then he drove me back to where I was staying.
>
> Soon after that, I had a strange dream about him. He was a soldier from some ancient country long ago. It was a hot, dry place. He held out one hand to me and put the other on his heart and said, 'You saved my life. One day, I will repay you.'

*That was the whole dream, but there was such a feeling
of gratitude in it, I think I might have done something for
him in a past life. This is why there's such a strong link
between us.*

*We've become good e-mail friends since then – we get on
so well. I'm going back there soon and we're going to meet
up again. I'm quite excited about it – it feels really good.*

An Ancient Promise

For all kinds of reasons, we sometimes have to say goodbye
to a place we love. As we look back for one last time and
whisper to ourselves, 'I will return,' we set in motion a vow
powerful enough to carry that wish until it's been fulfilled.

Even lifetimes later, we may feel driven to return
somewhere to heal a memory, make some kind of reparation
or complete unfinished business.

Harry's cousin had a job transfer to southern Germany
and invited Harry over there for a short holiday. Here is
what happened:

*I was doing all the usual sightseeing stuff. One day, I fetched
up outside an old convent. It was still in use as a nunnery.*

*I felt really drawn to it. There was a garden for visitors.
I sat there staring at the main building – and for some
reason I found myself wishing I could set all those nuns
free, as if they were doves in a cage. It brought up some
sad feelings. So I went into meditation for a while.*

*When I opened my eyes, there was a nun there looking at
me with her head on one side and a little smile. We got
talking. She was so friendly and sympathetic, I eventually
told her that for some strange reason, I felt like setting
them all free.*

She assured me that they weren't trapped – they were all very happy to be there, and could leave if they weren't. But she said she thought I needed to set something free anyway.

She told me that there was a girl staying with them who was a refugee from some war-torn area – she wouldn't say exactly where. In a few days, this girl's parents were coming to fetch her, as they'd finally managed to immigrate safely.

The nun – her name was Sister Marie – suggested that I be a part of this. Maybe that would give me the feeling of setting someone free from there.

I was quite excited about that. It felt good. I was due to go home the next day, but I extended my stay to be able to do this.

Sister Marie told me exactly what had to be done – there were various papers and protocols about it. Then she stood back and let me manage almost the whole thing myself.

The parents came to the nunnery, looking very apprehensive. When they saw their daughter safe and sound, there was the most beautiful reunion. They were all in tears. I was also sniffing and even Sister Marie was dabbing her eyes a bit. It was one of the most moving experiences I've ever had.

Harry underwent a regression to find out the deeper meaning of this experience and went back to a past life he'd had in that area.

It was in the early Middle Ages, a time of war and upheavals. He was one of the leaders, anxiously aware of how much danger his people were in from attackers on every side.

Because of the wars, his daughter was the only family he had left by then. So he made a decision: for her safety, he would put her into a convent. She was about 12 years old and not very happy about it.

He reassured her that it would only be temporary, and promised he'd come back for her when things had settled down. But within a year, he was killed in battle.

He realized it was guilt about breaking that promise that had come up again when he had visited the convent. This was why it had felt so good to reunite the refugee girl with her parents. Of course, he wondered if she was his daughter reincarnated.

He let me direct him to the Temple of Wisdom and Healing where he could talk this over with a spirit guide.

A guide came to him in the form of an angelic-looking nun. She told him that the refugee girl wasn't his previous daughter, but taking her from the convent was an important experience for him. It had set him free from his old guilt about breaking his promise to his daughter – who would now come back into his life. Harry asked who she'd be, but his guide only said he'd know when the time came.

The Gypsy Vow

Some of the vows we make are important for our long-term spiritual mission. As Vicky found, this can dovetail surprisingly well with conventional religious vows.

She recalled a life as a young woman in seventeenth-century England. She lived in a large mansion with her father and younger brother. It was run-down and shabby. The family's fortunes had gone down since the world had turned against them for being Catholics. Because of this, her life was overshadowed by a sense of helplessness. A dark cloud was hanging over her brother because the money for his schooling was running out. So she cheered herself up by going out to do nature sketches.

One fateful day she saw a couple of ragged children and started to draw them. Suddenly a rough man crept up behind her. She jumped up in fright, scattering all her art materials.

The man was a gypsy. These were his children and he seemed angry that she was drawing pictures of them. To appease him, she offered to do a drawing for him as payment for letting her draw the children.

At that, he pulled out a dagger. She was alarmed, but it turned out that he wanted her to draw a picture of it for him.

When she'd finished, he seemed satisfied. He pointed out the gypsies' camp and said she could come and draw them any time she wished.

Vicky was frightened by this encounter, but also excited. She decided not to tell her father about it in case he forbade her from going back there.

After that, she often went to the gypsy camp to draw the children, animals and caravans. She formed a wary friendship with the gypsies, taking them cheese or fruit and sharing the lunch-time stew they offered.

One day, one of the gypsy women offered to tell her fortune. As a good Catholic, Vicky was afraid of such things, but she decided it was just a bit of nonsense after all. For the sake of being friendly, she entered the woman's caravan.

She puts a crystal ball on the table and looks into it. She starts talking about a dagger... bloodshed... debts – not money debts, other kinds. I'm tied to it. I can't get away. I can't fight my fate. There are promises that must be kept. Dark shadows over the future. I must be true to something. I don't know what.

I don't really care. It's all rubbish anyway. I'm just waiting for her to stop. She does eventually.

Then, just as I'm going, she says she's seen that I can be trusted. And because of that, they'll soon start to tell me their secrets.

The gypsies were true to their word. They began explaining how their magic worked – but Vicky paid little attention to it. Eventually they found that what really interested her was their history. So they took her to a man who lived in the woods who could tell her more about it.

I'm with a skinny little gypsy man called Wizzle. He's taken me deep into the woods to a man's cottage. The man has dark hair. His name is Michael. It's a poor place, but he has books. He agrees to tell me what he knows.

After that Wizzle took me there quite often. They told me some strange things. It was all jumbled up, so I decided to write everything down when I got home. That way, I might make sense of it one day.

AF: *Can you remember any of it now?*

V: *Not in detail, but some things. The gypsies say they are descended from a wandering tribe of ancient Egyptians. That's where the word 'gypsy' comes from and why they know so much about magic.*

They believe they have a mission to keep this knowledge alive. According to their prophecies, one day their secret knowledge will go out into the world so everyone can know about it. But in the meantime, they have to be very careful. There are dark forces that want to destroy this knowledge altogether.

Then Vicky's life took an unexpected turn. Her father wanted her to marry a young man called Philip. He was well off and not Catholic, so the marriage would remove her family from both poverty and danger and her brother's schooling would be able to continue.

Vicky found Philip pleasant enough. But she'd secretly fallen in love with Michael, the man in the woods.

Despite everything that was at stake, her father didn't want to force her to do anything that would make her unhappy. So he gave her a week to decide.

In a turmoil of indecision, she went to ask the advice of the old family priest. Although overtly Church of England, he was covertly Catholic and knew how to keep the family's secrets. As they walked around the churchyard that chilly grey day, Vicky poured her heart out, telling him everything.

After some thought, the priest talked about the importance of duty over lower impulses. He asked Vicky to consider how she'd feel if she turned down this marriage and then had to watch her family continue to suffer.

That was enough to persuade her. She took the honourable course and married Philip.

Before the great day, she visited Michael to tell him the news. He seemed upset, but gave her an antique Egyptian scarab as a wedding gift.

Once married, she didn't have much time for drawing or visiting the gypsies, but she decided to go there one last time to say goodbye.

While she was there, her husband suddenly burst in, waving a gun around and accusing her of being unfaithful to him. Wizzle pulled her outside, bundled her onto her horse and told her to fly home as fast as she could.

Philip returned later with a knife wound in his arm. The doctor gave him sedatives to make him rest.

Vicky took the chance to try and explain that the only reason she'd visited the gypsies was to draw pictures and learn about their history. Philip refused to believe her, so to prove it she showed him her sketches and all the notes she'd made.

After that he went quiet. He locked her notes away, which she wasn't happy about, but at least he wasn't angry anymore.

A few months later he told her that someone important was coming to visit, who wanted to ask her some questions. All she knew was that he was something to do with a secret men's club.

He's quite old. Very courteous. He has a kindly manner. So it's not as bad as I thought. I answer all his questions.

AF: *What does he ask you?*

V: *About the gypsies. All the things they told me and showed me. At the end, he says he's going to take my papers and the scarab back to London. I'm not happy about that. But if it saves my marriage, then so be it.*

AF: *How does Phillip react to this?*

V: *I think it's put his mind at rest. I think he believes me now.*

(Several months later)

AF: *What happened to your papers and the scarab?*

V: *I don't know. I never saw them again. Philip refused to answer any of my questions about them, but as he was happy again I decided to let it all go and just be glad that the storm had passed.*

AF: *Did you ever see Michael or the gypsies again?*

V: *No. I never went back there.*

I suggested to Vicky that she went to the next time she heard any important news about her papers or the scarab.

Well, this is very strange. I'm not in that life anymore.
I'm in a place of blue light, with a – a spirit being. He's
emanating such a wonderful feeling. I feel more deeply
accepted and understood than I've ever felt before. I think
this must be an angel.

He – or she – is holding a white sphere. I somehow know I
should put my hands on it. So I do. As I do, the white mist in
the sphere starts to move around.

I'm looking into it now. Images are starting to form. I see
myself in another life before that life. I was a man, rough and
strong – I was a gypsy!

I am with three others. We have a dagger – a big fancy one. It
looks a bit like the dagger the man asked me to draw that day.
We use this dagger to cut a symbol into our arms. Then we
join hands above a fire. The blood from our wounds drips into
the fire. We're taking a blood oath. We are vowing to always
serve the secret purpose of the gypsy people, wherever that may
lead us.

The scene fades. The angel is sending thoughts into my mind
about it. He says that oath went very deep with me. It was
meant to last beyond that life, and it did. In the next life, even
when I was a Catholic girl, that vow unconsciously drove me
back to the gypsies again.

The angel is telling me that when I gave up my notes and
scarab to save my marriage, I worried – unconsciously – that
I had broken my sacred blood oath and betrayed the gypsies.
That worry has haunted me ever since – right up to this
lifetime. It's made me feel kind of guilty all the time. It's in
the background, but it's always there.

The angel is saying there's no reason to feel that guilt, because
I didn't break my vow. In fact, I fulfilled it. Even though

*I didn't understand it at the time, I was one of the people
destined to pass the gypsy knowledge on to where it would be
guarded safely – to people who would one day know exactly
how to leak bits of it out into the world.*

*The way that life turned out seemed a bit chaotic, but it was
exactly what was supposed to happen. So I didn't break my
vow to the gypsies after all.*

*The angel is now telling me about the dagger the gypsy
asked me to draw. That was a special sign to me, a coded
reminder of the blood oath that I'd taken. My subconscious
understood that.*

*He's saying that before we come into a life, we sometimes set
up this kind of signal for ourselves. When we get one of these
coded signs, it unconsciously sets us off on our mission.*

*When I saw the gypsy's dagger that day I knew deep down
what it meant – but in my heart, not my mind. It was a sign
of the path I was meant to follow. That's what really kept
me going back to the gypsies and taking all those risks. I was
following a deeper purpose than I could ever have understood
or accepted at the time. It was a purpose that was designed to
work with my Catholic faith, not against it.*

*That life took such strange twists. But I was following my true
mission all the time. It's a big relief to know that now.*

From personal decisions to grand declarations in a church,
past-life vows live on in our souls and have the power to
shape our lives and destinies. This is why negative vows –
vengeance, for example – are such a mistake. They turn into
heavy yokes on the spirit.

Perhaps we can't help making vows. In times of strong
emotion, it's a natural response to life. But this doesn't have
to be a bad thing. Negative vows come from hate, fear or

anger. Positive vows are based on love, hope or joy. This applies whether we make those vows in a church, a temple or simply to ourselves.

As long as they are positive, our spiritual vows and heartfelt decisions have the magical power to create happiness and fulfilment – not just in this life, but for many lifetimes to come.

Religion is like a giant tree. The branches are the different faiths, beliefs and philosophies. The leaves and flowers are the stories and symbols they use. These may change with the seasons of time, but the tree itself remains steadfast.

At first we may see only one branch of this tree, and assume this is all of it. Many wars have been fought over this illusion. Becoming aware of the different faiths we followed in our past lives will do much to establish freedom of belief and religious tolerance in the world.

What is the mystery at the centre of this mighty tree? Perhaps it's impossible to ever fully understand it, but I think it may be humanity's greater consciousness. This is why the faith that can move mountains always did come from within us.

YOUR PAST-LIFE MEMORIES OF RELIGIOUS MAGIC

Once again, this visualization will introduce you to your past-life memories in a safe and gentle way. You'll be able to view scenes from your past lives as a detached observer, without needing to relive any of the experiences. Whenever you wish, you can stop the exercise simply by opening your eyes. For extra reassurance, ask your guardian angel or spirit guide to be with you.

Repeat this exercise whenever it feels right. At first you may get only brief glimpses of your memories, but with practice you'll gather a lot of information about your past lives. As you go along, you'll begin to see the bigger picture of your soul's reincarnational journey. This will help you to understand much more about your current life and how it fits into your higher purpose.

- ◎ *Preparation:* Sit or lie somewhere where you can be quiet and undisturbed.

- ◎ *Relaxation:* Scrunch up and expand all your muscles – especially your face, hands, arms and shoulders. Then let all your muscles soften and relax.

- ◎ *Focus:* Become aware of everything that's underneath you. Sense how comfortable, firm and supportive it is.

- ◎ *Centre yourself:* Gaze steadily at a candle or a crystal until you want to close your eyes.

- ◎ *Clear your mind:* Breathe slowly and deeply, right down to your stomach. Listen to the sound of your breath.

- ◎ *Approach the gateway:* Imagine that you're waiting at the foot of a hill. Soon a white-robed figure comes towards you. They lead you up a path that spirals around the hill.

- ◎ *The doorway:* At the top, you enter a simple but beautiful temple. In the centre is a pool with a fountain. Your guide fills a ceremonial goblet with the water and hands it to you. This water holds the benefits of your religious past lives. You drink as much of it as you wish.

- ◎ *Observe and explore:* Your guide bids you to look into the pool. As you gaze into it, you see scenes from your past lives. Let them unfold and watch for as long as you wish.

- ◎ *Cleanse yourself:* Dip your hands into the water and sprinkle it over your face and head. This will help to cleanse and heal any inner wound you may have received during your religious past lives.

 Return: When you want to leave, thank your guide and bid farewell. Return gently and smoothly to your everyday surroundings.

❖ ❖ ❖

PART III
SECRET SOCIETIES

'We dance round in a ring and suppose,
But the secret sits in the middle and knows.'
Robert Frost

INTRODUCTION

A new Freemason about to be initiated is ordered at sword point to strip down to his underpants. His watch, rings and any other sign of identity or status must also go. He has to wear a rough, pyjama-like outfit and roll up the right sleeve and left trouser leg. As a final touch, his escort yanks back the top to expose the left side of his chest.

Thus stripped of dignity, blindfolded by the 'hoodwink' and with a noose around his neck, the candidate is led before the assembled lodge.

A long and arcane ceremony follows. One of its high points is the vow of secrecy. The candidate has to swear that if he ever betrays his oath he can expect to 'have my throat rent asunder, my tongue forcibly removed and my worthless body buried on such a part of a beach where the tide doth ebb and flow'.

The ceremony concludes with the words: 'The sacred promise you have entered into this evening will bind your conscience for as long as you shall live.'

Bloodcurdlingly binding vows of secrecy are not exclusive to Freemasonry. Most clandestine groups have powerful entry rituals. Dion Fortune said the Golden Dawn initiation was designed to 'produce the most remarkable psychic experiences and extensions of consciousness in those who had any psychic capacity at all'.

Like the techniques of brainwashing, initiations first isolate and then disorientate the candidate. Blindfolding is a common practice, with extra confusions thrown in. These procedures loosen the initiate's hold on their sense of identity and everyday reality. Their mind is then open to receive information and instructions at subliminal levels, unprotected by the usual mental guards and filters.

Powerful archetypal symbols, solemn ritual and a sense of danger all make a deep impression on the subconscious mind. Vows sworn under these conditions are likely to be kept - sometimes well beyond that lifetime. This severe level of secrecy was vital in the days when careless talk could reap terrible consequences.

Another reason esoteric groups value secrecy is because it protects the neophyte. The special knowledge of each initiatory level is shielded, so that questors move to the next stage only when they're ready for it. This also stops outsiders picking up bits of knowledge or powers that they might abuse. These have been the traditional ways of occult schools all over the world, dating as far back as ancient Egypt and India.

Vast stores of advanced knowledge from those earlier times were lost when the Library of Alexandria was burned down. After that, mystery schools and spiritual groups like the Essenes and the Gnostics kept alight the flickering lamps of the old wisdom.

This custodianship later passed to medieval esoteric societies. Because the Church had banned any knowledge outside official doctrine, those groups used coded symbols to protect themselves.

The Knights of the Swan, for example, chose that emblem because it represented the fully developed pineal gland – the third eye. This gives us the ability to visualize, and also to see beyond material reality. In modern humans it has atrophied to the size of a pea. But with meditation and practice, it can grow again. In certain medieval circles, the swan stood for this secret quest.

Esoteric wisdom from Persia and Arabia later found its way into medieval Europe through the Knights Templar. Knowing the authorities would do all they could to stamp it out, the Templars guarded this knowledge with their secret code, the Atbash Cipher, which was later found in the Dead Sea scrolls. They also encoded their secrets into the design and carvings of their great Gothic cathedrals.

Most people who are attracted to higher knowledge have spent at least one life on these long and winding trails of hidden history. The exciting combination of danger and secrecy leaves a lasting impression on the psyche, making this an important part of any soul's journey.

On the downside, living like this can create a paranoia which may persist beyond that lifetime. People sometimes find themselves unwittingly re-creating lives of concealment and duplicity because the inner self still feels that it's necessary. Understanding where that comes from helps to melt away these left-over effects.

GETTING PAST THE SECRECY GUARD

A vow of secrecy taken in an earlier life may continue to restrict you long after it has become irrelevant. One of the most effective ways to deal with this kind of issue is at the symbolic level. When you do that, it's like changing the deep inner settings that unconsciously define the scope of your experiences.

This kind of vow acts like an unyielding sentry, barring the door to any memories of your experiences in secret societies and the special knowledge that you might have gained during those lives.

A good way to deal with this is to visualize a locked door with a sentinel standing in front of it. Then:

◎ Talk to this guard. Ask him why he's there.

◎ Tell him that the old orders have changed. His new orders are to let you in, and to be supportive and helpful to you from now on.

◎ Keep on until he finally opens the door for you.

Notice all the details, because they'll be full of clues about this exciting chapter in your soul's history. For example:

◎ What sort of time period did this seem to be in?

◎ How would you describe the guard?

◎ What did the door look like?

◎ When you got in, what kind of place did you find?

Once you're through the door, you may find a symbol of knowledge and wisdom, such as a crystal sphere, a treasure chest or an owl. Whatever you discover there will have special significance for you, with good clues about your past lives. You can stay there to explore and investigate for as long as you wish.

When you feel ready, thank the guard for his help and return gently to your everyday world. From now on it'll be much easier to access memories and knowledge that were once mysteriously unavailable to you.

A happy outcome of secret society lives is the enduring friendships they create. Your comrades in the cause may have felt as close as family. This creates strong bonds that can last for lifetimes. Does anyone you know come to mind? If so, it could be a clue about your former quests together.

Secret societies aren't always officially organized groups. In medieval and Renaissance times, free-thinkers belonged to a looser-knit community of people who understood one another through other kinds of secrecy. Outside the strict walls of Church dogma there frolicked a rich world of colourful codes and symbols.

Fairytales are full of them, expressing once unorthodox ideas in the form of stories. *Sleeping Beauty* was about finding your inner spirit. *Jack and the Beanstalk* dramatized the importance of following your heart. *Beauty and the Beast* showed the transformational power of love.

Colour coding was often central to these tales. The description of 'cheeks pale as the snow, lips red as blood, and hair as black as the raven's wing' was really a sly reference to alchemy. These colours were about the stages of turning lead to gold – which itself was a secret metaphor for spiritual transformation.

The Tarot cards encoded huge volumes of secret esoteric teachings. The Church especially disliked the High Priestess card because it stood for female spiritual authority.

One of the biggest symbols of the time was the rose. It stood for secrecy, the spiritual path and love. Renaissance heretics turned love into a form of worship. They venerated the feminine, raising women above the lowly status the Church had dished out to them. In the courtly circles of high-born heretics, devotion to a particular lady became a form of religion.

An even riskier heresy grew from this: the celebration of erotic love as a spiritual path. But this was no hippie lovefest.

An admirer had to get through a lot of noble deeds and pining before his lady even looked at him. Eventually she might favour him with her scarf, which was carefully colour coded. He'd then wear it in ways that sent silent messages to her about his love.

Troubadours, poets and storytellers of the time entertained the courts of Europe with tales and songs that were full of double meaning. They loaded their works with coded messages meant only for the cognoscenti.

One troubadour said of his poem: 'Thou can'st go whither thou wilt. I have dressed thee so well that thou will be understood by those endowed with intelligence: of others thou need'st not be concerned.'

In all these ways the secret underground world developed a rich culture of signs, smokescreens and red herrings. This was called the Language of the Birds or the Green Language.

As a result, a cornucopia of vibrant symbols pours out from those times to us now. For the many who belonged to that world, they whisper tales of colourful memories that are just waiting for rediscovery.

15

MYSTERY SCHOOLS

The Egyptian mystery schools were famous, especially the Temple of Waset at Luxor, which was the world's first university. People flocked there from around the world. All the major Greek philosophers spent at least ten years there – Pythagoras, Socrates, Plato, Euclid, Hippocrates, Archimedes and Euripides – as did numerous lesser-known names.

Pythagoras studied there for 22 years. He also learned from the Magis of Mesopotamia, Indian Brahmins and British Druids. When he returned to southern Italy, he set up a mystery school to teach others what he'd learned. He was inspired by the ambition to turn Greece into another Egypt, where the rulers would be guided by lofty spiritual principles.

His most famous disciple was Plato, who'd also studied in Egypt. Like Pythagoras, he tried to spread this wisdom to others. Some saw him as the incarnation of Apollo, but many others attacked him. In the classical world, only a minority was interested in this kind of knowledge. Those in power actively opposed it.

In 399BCE Socrates was sentenced to death by hemlock for 'corrupting the youth' with these ideas. Plato and Aristotle realized what that meant for them and fled Athens.

Open teaching was clearly too dangerous. To survive, the mystery schools learned to make sure that nothing slipped out about them. As a result, we know very little about their inner workings.

The most famous of these schools was at Eleusis. Here they used dramatic rituals to make people directly aware of the true nature of life and death. They believed that participating in these allegorical dramas helped to awaken the soul's fuller consciousness. The experiences were also designed to prepare people for the underworld – their final passage through it and perhaps also some interactions along the way.

Initiates to the Lesser Mysteries went through a metaphorical journey: Demeter's descent into Hades, searching for her lost child Persephone. This represented the descent of spirit into matter, the sense of loss that created and the search to find the inner self again.

Initiation to the Greater Mysteries was more elaborate. It began with several days of fasting, purification and seclusion. Then, carrying boughs of myrtle, with myrtle leaf wreaths on their heads, the candidates filed down the Sacred Road to Eleusis.

At the first bridge they had a ritual drink of water infused with roasted barley, pennyroyal and, many think, some kind of psychoactive herb.

Several other ceremonies punctuated the long procession. By the time the candidates approached Eleusis, night was falling and torches lit the way. Waiting for them inside the first gate, sitting on a throne, was the hierophant – the high priest.

Nobody knows what happened after that. The rest of the proceedings was completely secret. Anyone who tried to talk about them was swiftly silenced. Some say a brilliant light sometimes shone out for miles around. Others say the symbol of a grain kernel was somehow important. But to this day we know little more than that about the Eleusian Mysteries. Even our past-life memories are curiously guarded about them.

When she made an appointment for a regression, Beth e-mailed me about a recurring dream she had that sounded like this kind of initiation:

> In these dreams, I'm always wearing a long white dress. I'm sometimes holding things, but it's never clear exactly what. I go into a big place. Then it gets weird. Different things happen. Sometimes there's a very powerful person there who grows into a giant. Sometimes the place gets filled with coloured light. But the dreams always end around then.

Before her regression we set the intention for her to access more about this memory if that would be beneficial for her.

At first she saw nothing but swirling colours. Then the light slowly took on the form of a beautiful being. It told Beth it was the inner knowledge she'd gained during her time in the mystery schools of ancient Greece. It would always be part of her. It was the source of her good intuition and the psychic abilities that she should trust and use more than she did. But the time had not yet come for her to access any more memories about her initiations. This was partly because the highest revelations were given to initiates when they were in a profoundly altered state of mind. These understandings didn't translate well into the words of everyday thinking – it would betray them to even try.

Although it was not yet time for her to see any more, one day the time would come. When that happened, it would be hugely beneficial.

The message ended with the light being enfolding Beth in translucent colours and transmitting an extra gift to her: greater trust in her psychic powers.

Afterwards Beth said that was perfect – it was what she'd really needed. Her distrust of her abilities had been holding her back for a long time.

'I have a feeling that I'm meant to find my way to these memories by using my own mind somehow,' she said. 'It's something to do with meditation. This feels great. It's put me on a whole new path.'

The Eleusian Mystery rituals continued until the fourth century CE. By then the Christian Roman Emperor Valentinian was trying to ban pagan ceremonies, but without great success. The newly Christianized Visigoths finished that job for him when they invaded in 396, looting and trashing all the pagan centres. Eleusis was completely destroyed.

The Wisdom-Keeper

Past lives from those turbulent times can sometimes make us nervous about secret teachings. But they may also inspire a strong dedication to study forbidden knowledge and keep it alive. In his regression, Ethan went back to a life in Greece in which he became growingly aware of the dangers of that time.

The memory began with him standing on the balcony of his house, high on a hill overlooking the sea. He felt that he came from a Middle Eastern country and his wife was Greek. They were happy together, sharing a glass of wine and enjoying the sunset. But all was not well.

My wife wants to cancel a little dinner party we've planned. It's because of something our spiritual teacher told us. He said the world was going to get darker. This came from the mystery school where he teaches. They have ways of knowing things like that.

AF: *Do you go to that school?*

E: *We don't go there, but he comes and teaches us here at home. He's like family to us. We call him Grandfather. He says it'll be hundreds of years before things really change, but we'll start to see the signs of it now.*

My wife says she doesn't trust some of our old friends anymore. I reassure her, so she agrees to go ahead with the party, but I know she's still worried.

It's deep twilight now. The evening star has come out. We stand there arm in arm, just looking at it together.

The memory shifted to the time of the party:

There's a low table in the middle of the room with lots of food and drink on it. We sit or lie on cushions on the floor. Everybody just helps themselves when they feel like it. There are flowers everywhere. Somebody's playing a flute.

It's a warm night. The doorway is open to the balcony. I put our big pots of flowers near the doorway so the scent will come into the room. I love these evenings that we have.

Everyone is laughing, but I'm not. They're making jokes about people like Grandpa. I don't like that.

A bit earlier, my wife suddenly left the room. I tried to follow her, but she shook her head.

(Pause)

Now it's the end of the evening. Our guests have gone home and we're sitting on the balcony. My wife is telling me that she left the room because she overheard mocking remarks about us. She says it's not the first time she's heard those people talk like that, but she didn't want to tell me.

I feel so angry. She was right: it really is time to stop these parties.

(A few days later)

We're with Grandpa, sitting in the sun outside, sharing bread and honey. My wife says she doesn't go to the market by the seashore anymore because it's been taken over by rough people.

Grandpa says gangs of robbers have started roaming the countryside. Then he puts a scroll on the table.

I pick it up. It's in a strange language.

Grandpa says it's full of secrets from old Egypt. He says there are other books like this. His school has made it their mission to find them and keep them safe. He asks if we'd like to help them do that.

I am very keen. I look at my wife to see how she feels about it. She smiles and nods. I tell him we'll be happy to do this work.

It takes me out of the sadness I was feeling about my old friends. I have a new purpose in life now.

The couple devoted the rest of their lives to collecting books of secret wisdom for the mystery school. Ethan travelled all over the Mediterranean and Egypt to find them.

I had some adventures doing that. The most dramatic one was in Alexandria. There was a wealthy book collector there. He'd somehow found out about me. He knew I was looking for certain books.

His manservant approached me in the street and told me his master had a special book for me. It could have been a trap, but I decided to take a chance and went with the servant.

When we got there, I could see this was the house of a wealthy man. It was covered with a creeper that was full of purple flowers. Once we were inside, I had to wait in a beautiful indoor courtyard. It had a fountain and a lot of green plants.

After a while, the servant came back with a message from his master inviting me to share supper with him. I was shown to a room full of rich carpets and cushions. My host was a short, plump, merry sort of man.

As the evening went by, I started to feel very strange. It turned out he'd put some kind of truth drug in my food. I ended up telling him a lot of secrets that I shouldn't have. Then I passed out.

In the morning I woke up alone in the same room. I had a terrible headache. The servant came in with a pot of coffee and some pastries, but I refused to eat anything else there.

He then gave me a leather bag and said it was a gift from his master.

Inside the bag there was a really important book. It was one we'd despaired of ever finding – a real prize. It turned out that my host had given me the truth drug to test me. He needed to be sure that I wasn't a spy.

When I got home, Grandpa was overjoyed with the book. He said he knew that man from long ago and he really was one of us.

(Pause)

I'm much older now. I'm standing on our high veranda, looking out to sea. Grandpa passed on many years ago, but his spirit is often with me.

He's my guide in this life as well. He's with me now. He says it's time for me to understand that our mission was a success. If we hadn't done that work, the world would have become a much bleaker place. The secret teachings and books that we and others preserved made all the difference. They were real lights in a darkening world.

After the regression, Ethan commented that books had always been lucky for him. Once, when he was desperate, out of the blue he had landed a good job in a bookshop. Whenever he needed to know something, the right book invariably presented itself. When he'd become interested in New Age thought, he'd always felt strongly guided to the perfect book to read next.

I avoid using the word 'karma' because for so many it's come to mean punishment. From what I've seen, karma is real enough, but it works in a far more profound and benign way than as an agent of simple retribution. It sounds to me as though Ethan's past-life deeds earned him the good karma of a happy relationship with books.

Our past-life memories of mystery schools may be elusive, but the knowledge and accomplishments we gained in those schools remain within us, and may still be enhancing our lives in all kinds of unexpected ways.

16

INITIATION

I nitiation into a secret society is a watershed moment. Afterwards, nothing can be the same again. This is because initiations are all about symbolic death and rebirth. They mark the end of the old identity and its way of thinking and the birth of a more enlightened self. In Freemasonry the fresh initiate is called an ashlar: a rough stone to be shaped with esoteric training.

Another traditional purpose of initiation is to show the candidate that death is an illusion. For this reason, the rituals mimic as closely as possible the experience of dying and then returning to life.

In shamanic initiations the old self is said to be torn apart and put back together again with new magical powers. This can mean some tough physical tests. Many tribal cultures mark the successful initiate with a pattern of cuts deep enough to make permanent scars. These marks are often on the face to show the world the person's triumph over painful trials and their new status in the community.

Certain Druid initiations were a truly life-or-death test. They placed the candidate like a corpse into a coffin-like canoe. Then they pushed it out to sea, to drift where it would. Those who survived and returned to shore had passed the test.

In his regression, Steven recalled a similar experience:

I was walking slowly up a hill, in single file with a line of Druids. A big hood covered my head. I was meant to keep my eyes on the ground.

I'd just been through some really tough initiation tests. I could only remember feeling a lot of pain and then becoming unconscious, so I didn't know if I'd passed or not.

As we processed up the hill, the others were chanting in low, deep voices. It made me feel doomed.

Then, when we reached the sacred place, they stood me in the centre of their circle. Someone pulled my hood off and told me to look up.

Standing in front of me was the leader of the group. He had a wreath in his hands and he was smiling at me. They all began to sing a song of triumph and joy and the leader stepped forward and placed the wreath on my head. It meant I was now one of them.

Tears were pouring down my face. It was the biggest moment of my life.

Initiations in the Middle East could be just as gruelling. Anyone wishing to join certain mystery schools there had to go through a form of crucifixion. In his initiation, the famous magician Apollonius of Tyana hung on a cross until he was unconscious. He was then laid in the sarcophagus inside the Great Pyramid for three days. During that time he said his spirit left his body and accessed higher realms of consciousness.

In medieval Europe, initiation was thought of as a journey to the Invisible Magic Mountain. Strange beasts lay in wait there to test the candidate. Heraldic and alchemical creatures like the green lion, unicorn, phoenix, pelican or eagle represented these trials. They stood for challenging aspects of the self that would come up to try and send the initiate back. A successful initiation meant facing and dealing with them.

An initiation from any era is a major experience. It leaves an indelible impression on the psyche. Its key symbols will be significant to the inner self from that lifetime on. In later lives, those symbols may return to us as gifts, or items that come into our lives with seemingly magical ease. They will ring a bell and feel somehow special. When this happens, it's a sign that we're ready to reconnect with our past-life awareness from that time.

When a friend's son, Pete, was preparing for his first job interview, he came home with a curious tie-pin he'd found that looked like a griffin. Despite his mother's reservations, he was determined to wear it to the interview, feeling sure it would bring him luck.

A griffin is part serpent, part bird and part lion. This is a code standing for specific powers gained through years of esoteric training. Perhaps it stirred Pete's memories of a life when this symbol meant much more than a lucky talisman.

The interview did go well and he got the job. A few months later, a new friend at that workplace told him about an esoteric society that he belonged to. Pete was immediately attracted and jumped at the invitation to join.

He feels it is the best decision he's ever made and he's convinced that his griffin somehow brought him this good fortune.

The Brotherhood of the Rose

Sometimes a past-life initiation goes so deep it can even create physical effects in this life. When Omar came to see me, he'd had chest surgery about a year before. Since then he'd noticed that he felt oddly pleased whenever he looked at the surgical scars on his chest. He had also started having recurring dreams about people in historical dress cutting him. So he decided to have a regression to see if he could unearth what that was all about.

His memory went back to a time when he'd been beaten up and left for dead in the street. He'd been a young Italian man, a bit of a hothead, and had courted danger by speaking out too freely against the Pope. He felt that this had taken place during Renaissance times. His name had been Ricardo.

Floating a bit above his body, expecting death any moment, he had the vague impression that a carriage had stopped and picked him up. The next thing he remembered was waking up in a huge bed in a luxurious room.

He was in great pain and a doctor was attending to him. Soon his best friend, Lorenchio, joined them. He told Ricardo that they'd found him lying in the street and had brought him back to his wealthy family's home. They were going to do all they could to save his life.

Slowly, Ricardo recovered. After a while, he felt it was time to go back to his comparatively humble rooms in town.

I'm in a big chair in the garden with a blanket around me. Lorenchio is sitting with me. I'm worried about some anti-Pope papers that I hid in my rooms. I want to go back and see if they're still there, but Lorenchio says he has something to tell me.

He says my rooms were ransacked. Everything I had was destroyed, so they will have found those papers. I'm sure that's what they were looking for.

I start saying silent prayers to the angel of death: 'Come soon, come soon. Let me not be a burden to these people anymore.'

(A few days later)

I now have a new hope in life. Lorenchio told me that he was my friend because his family had the same attitudes that I did. But with them it went much deeper.

He told me that they belonged to a special society called the Brothers of the Rose, with powerful secret knowledge that the Church had forbidden the people. It was high wisdom from very long ago. I wanted to know what it was, but he said I could only find out if I joined them.

He said there were many secret societies. They looked different but they all had a common purpose. This was to guard and preserve the secret traditions – to keep the hidden knowledge alive.

I asked why it had to be kept secret. Why couldn't they just tell everybody about these things? He said the times were still too dangerous for that, but the brotherhoods were preparing. One day they would bring the secret knowledge into the open.

He said these societies ran in families. That was because rich and powerful families could do more or less as they pleased and nobody would challenge them. But the only way I would find out more was by joining them...

In the months following, Ricardo began doing odd jobs for the family, moved into a cottage in the grounds of their house and decided to join their secret society. He was very excited when the time came for his initiation:

When it was near to midnight Lorenchio took me outside, to the entrance of their garden maze. I was blindfolded. They say that without their secret knowledge you don't have full sight. When they take the blindfold off, you'll see what was hidden before.

Lorenchio led me into the maze. I could feel that there were a few others there, but not many. I had to kneel down. I could hear them moving to certain places around me.

Then they started a kind of chant and I felt as though I was being bound. I thought they were passing a rope between them that was wrapping around me, but I later found out that they did that only with their words. It was to seal me in.

They challenged me with some strange questions. Lorenchio had already told me the answers I had to give. Then they took the blindfold off me. I had to take a blood oath of secrecy.

They used the thorn of a rose to scratch a symbol over my heart. They said they would carve this symbol right into my heart with a sword if I ever betrayed their society. One of the men took a few drops of my blood and placed it on a special seal of their symbol.

When it was all done, they embraced me and welcomed me into their brotherhood. They said they would now pass on the teachings of the first stage to me.

When I'm ready I'll go through the second and then the third and final stage of the initiation. That will be in front of the whole brotherhood, in their secret meeting-place. Until then I'm not allowed to know who they all are.

After that, Ricardo felt on top of the world. He was living in a beautiful place with like-minded people and they were training him on a special path of spiritual development. He applied himself enthusiastically and it became his central purpose in life.

He expected to go through the next stage of his initiation quite soon after the first. But it didn't happen. He wondered if he was being blocked for some reason. When he asked his friend what he was doing wrong, Lorenchio always said he'd find out, but no answer ever came back. After a while, his already fragile health began to go down:

> *I'm in bed in the luxurious room where I first woke up here. I'm very ill. I was never well after that beating – always aches and pains, colds and ailments. This time I don't think I'll recover.*

AF: *Why do you say that?*

O: *It's the way they whisper together. Also... I just know, somehow. I think I've lost heart in life.*

I was so excited about joining the brotherhood and I worked so hard at it, but I've made no progress with it. It's been the same for a few years, so I've given up on it. The joy it once gave me has all gone now.

(A few days later)

I'm close to the end, but I feel much happier than I have for a long time.

Lorenchio came to speak to me when no one else was around. It was like the old days when we were good friends.

He said he knew that I'd been unhappy about the brotherhood. It had hurt him to see that and not be able to do anything about it or to explain anything, so now he was going to tell me why I had been held back.

He said it was because senior members of the society kept voting against me. It wasn't him or his father or the doctor – they all wanted me to continue – but the other men in the society were the ones who made this kind of decision.

I asked why they had voted against me.

He said it was because when I was younger I'd talked too much. So they'd decided I couldn't be trusted with their secrets and I was never to go beyond the first stage – which was only a preparation. The real secrets didn't come till later.

Then he said that because I was ill – dying, really – he was now going to tell me some of those secrets.

He said that everyone's soul definitely lived on after death. It returned to life after life in different bodies. That went on for thousands of years, until we were advanced enough to move on to higher worlds.

That was new to me. I thought we had only one life and when we died we went to heaven or hell.

He also told me about certain people who could live in the same body for an amazingly long time. They had a secret that was very well guarded.

I felt that I needed to rest to consider these things. This new information was churning around inside me like something too big to digest. But Lorenchio went on talking. He said that some of the secret societies trained certain people to have the power to stay alive and healthy for much longer than normal. Those people kept the brotherhoods going. They built on the knowledge and continued the work.

Very few people could do that. More were trained to return in their next life to the same family and continue the work in that way. They died at the normal time and then reincarnated – but they came back with this special intent and purpose. There were certain powerful families who had used this secret to make themselves very strong.

He said there wasn't time to train me to do that, but we could make a pact to meet again in another life. Whenever we met, we'd be friends and help each other.

I felt very happy about this. We joined hands and just had time to make the pledge. Then someone came in and we had to stop talking about these things.

My mind was reeling. My heart was full. I vowed that, God willing, in my lives to come I would find a way to carry on up the initiation ladder. That talk with Lorenchio gave me hope again.

I could let go of that life then. It was time to go. I left in peace.

There was a long pause, while Omar quietly accessed more information. Afterwards he told me that during that time he'd seen glimpses of himself in two later lives:

I was in some kind of secret society in America. The War of Independence was just round the corner. We were plotting for it and stirring people up. We knew how important it was to break away from the British. It felt good to be doing that. It gave me the chance to use up all my political anger and do something active to change things for the better.

Then I saw myself in another life. I was dressed like a Victorian gentleman. I was at a meeting – it looked like the Freemasons. By then I wasn't such a hothead. I was more into the esoteric stuff.

I got the impression those two lives fulfilled my need for secret societies to accept me and to do all the degrees of initiation I wanted, with nobody trying to stop me – my need to make up for that life in Italy and feel OK about myself again.

But none of that attracts me anymore. Maybe because I've been there, done that, in this life I've been looking for something beyond secret societies.

I asked Omar if he had ever been back to that house in Italy or seen his friend from there again. He sensed that was still to come. When the time was right, he was going to return in triumph in some way, without any of his old need to be accepted by that society.

He also realized why he felt good about his surgical scars: they reminded him of the symbol that had been scratched on his chest with a rose thorn so long ago. It was the sign of his first initiation – and the beginning of his journey through the world of secret societies. He felt that it had returned to show him he'd passed another initiation – to let him know that he'd now graduated from the clandestine world. From now on, his spiritual path would be guided by his intuition, inner knowing and the special teachings of his own soul.

17

THE LONG-TERM MISSION

As Omar discovered in his short time with the Brotherhood of the Rose, esoteric societies tend to have a long-term mission. This is usually about transforming humanity, so it's a purpose that will take many lifetimes.

In the days when even believing in reincarnation was dangerous heresy, these people had advanced secret knowledge about how to use it to make sure they'd return to the same group and continue their work there. Although Omar never heard exactly how they did this, it probably included a dramatic ritual designed to impress this intention as deeply as possible into the subconscious. This would be a formal, conscious way of doing what people do naturally all the time.

While our bodies sleep at night, our astral selves automatically head for whatever interests us the most. We do much the same thing when we finally leave the body at the end of this life.

In his pioneering books about out-of-body experiences, Robert Monroe explained what we do and where we go when the body has died. One of his first discoveries was that newly departed souls could be quite disorientated. They often didn't understand that they weren't in their physical body anymore and would stubbornly cling to their old haunts. So he began helping these confused souls to let go and move on. As he did, he noticed a strange trend: just as he was leading a spirit towards the higher realms, they'd suddenly disappear. Troubled by this, he explored further until he'd solved the mystery.

He found that the astral realms contained myriads of different areas and levels of consciousness. Every religion and belief system had its own region, some of which could be vast. As well as those sectors, there were also higher spiritual planes and zones of low vibration.

Monroe realized that as he was taking souls past the places that were closest to their own vibration and beliefs, they'd automatically be drawn into them. That was why they suddenly disappeared: they were going to the afterlife heavens of their chosen religions.

We're attracted to future incarnations in much the same way. Our deep beliefs and general vibration will draw us towards the experiences that are in tune with them. Being deeply immersed in a secret society acts like a natural magnet. If our feelings about it are unchanged, the next time we incarnate it will pull us naturally back towards it. A conscious decision to do this will make it much more certain.

Secret societies aren't the only souls to make this kind of choice. All kinds of groups may decide to reincarnate at the same time to follow a particular mission. It's a common belief in Nigeria that this happens all the time.

Shared endeavours may also be planned in the between-life worlds. Perhaps the most secret society of all is the one that's formed before its members reincarnate. Once in the physical world, they may never join clubs or societies, or even meet each other, but the strong unconscious bond of their mission will be updated and maintained in the dream state.

Their purpose may be more far-reaching than they realize while they are here. For example, in the 1930s Edgar Cayce predicted that large numbers of Atlanteans would start to incarnate in the second half of the twentieth century, mostly in America. Many of them would bring their ancient technological expertise and continue developing it for the good of the world. They would also bring old issues around inequality to be redressed and healed. Their way would be one of fervour – even extremism at times. I think most people would agree that this is exactly what unfolded from the 1960s onwards.

Perhaps all spiritually focused societies, clubs and associations have deeper roots in the between-life worlds. According to nineteenth-century occultist Alice Bailey's spirit guide, 'Freemasonry is a terrestrial version of an initiatory school that exists on Sirius. The various hierarchical degrees of Freemasonry are parallels of the different levels of initiation that an adept must go through in order to enter the greater lodge on Sirius.'

As long as they remain content with the same belief system, people will naturally reincarnate back into their favourite milieu. Reincarnated Druids, pagans and Wiccans are almost certainly the driving force behind the modern revivals of those ways.

A Wiccan I know was utterly miserable in her slick modern flat. She was happy only when she'd moved to a tumble-down old cottage where she could hang herbs from the rafters and have a real fire. She said she could be her real self again there.

A Druid friend told me about an insight he'd received during one of their ceremonies. They were all standing in a circle. At a quiet moment, he sensed that behind each of them stood a taller, older Druid. He said it felt as though they were there to guide and watch over them – and that they'd been doing this for centuries.

When we belong to any spiritually oriented group, our personal path weaves around that group's long-term purpose and interacts with it in ways that create the dramas of our lives. Sometimes that can take us down completely unexpected paths.

The Green Ring

Gemma dreamed that she found an antique green ring that she'd loved but lost a long time ago. The dream was so vivid that she decided to have a past-life regression to find out more. She went back to the life of a happy young woman at a French château around Renaissance times.

> They're all quite elegant here. It's like a little court. I think I'm the daughter of someone who has some sort of... not exactly work... some sort of function here. Not a servant, though – we have good status.

> I'm in the garden, walking and talking with a man. I'm a bit wary of him. He's quite attractive. I like his voice and his eyes. But he says strange things.

> He's taking his leave now. I hold out my hand and he kisses my ring. He says that ring is special. It's got a green stone in the centre and little pearls around it. It's my favourite. But he doesn't know that.

Afterwards Gemma said it was the same ring she'd seen in her dream. The strange man came back and seemed to be courting her. She enjoyed that, but some of the things he said disturbed her.

One day, to illustrate a point he was making, he drew a pentagram on the ground. She reacted badly:

> This is an evil sign! I stamp on it till it's gone. It's the sign of the devil.

> He's not pleased. He says he must leave now and never return. I don't want that to happen. I tell him that I want to see him but I don't want this – this heresy. He says that heresy is the secret truth.

> I feel shocked and frightened. I ask him if he's the devil. He just laughs. Then he says I must decide. If I want to see him again, he'll tell me more about these things. If I don't want to hear them, he'll go now and never return.

> I don't know what to do. But I like him. So I say it would please me to see him again. I've started to call him the Shadowman.

After that, the man continued to visit her, slowly gaining her confidence and drawing her into his purpose.

> There's an underground group of people like him. They have plans to change the world for the better. He wants me to join them and help them.

> It's night-time. I'm at a secret meeting with him and another man. We're in a cottage a few miles away from my home. The candle's making big jumping shadows on the walls.

> They want to know if I will help them. I say, 'What can I do?' They say they want me to marry one of the men in their society.

> Oh, how I wish it could be the Shadowman! But it's impossible anyway. My father has already chosen someone for me to marry and his mind is made up. I tell them that. They just say they'll find a way round it. I can't see how, though.

But in the end they did find a way. The man they wanted her to marry, Bertrand, became her father's advisor on gardening matters. Their shared interest in orchards eventually bore important fruit: the wedding of Gemma to Bertrand.

She was happy because she felt this would bring her closer to the fascinating Shadowman and his secret world, but as time went by she found the opposite took place: she felt increasingly ignored by the group. And as her resentment grew, her husband became more distant. This eventually came to a head:

> One day when I was feeling down I told Bertrand that I thought they were all in league with the devil. After that he stopped telling me about their secret things. But I don't care. I don't want to hear about that stuff anymore.

> **AF:** *Do you still support their aims?*

> **G:** *Oh, their aims! I know what their real aims are: they plan to take over all the lands of France. Marrying me was part of that plan. It was just to get my property. They talk about serving the Queen of Heaven, but they've used me like a pawn.*

> (The memory moved on to the end of that life.)

> I'm much older now. In bed. Dying. People are around the bed. It's near the end... I can feel myself slipping out of my body... Now I'm out – it was easier than I thought. I'm floating slowly upwards.

> I'm in a beautiful place now. An angel has been helping me to understand things. They are kind and gentle about everything here. But I still feel disappointed in myself.

> I allowed myself to get so bitter. The angel is showing me that it didn't have to turn out the way it did. It was more up to

me than I realized. I could have been more involved with that group right through my life.

But it's alright – I'm going to have another life to make up for it. I'll do it properly next time.

We moved to the life that had been planned to complete that unfinished business. Gemma found herself a young woman in 1930s England. Rumours of war were in the air. Very keen to do her bit, she joined the armed services and started working her way towards becoming a spy.

Once she'd passed all the tests, she began serious training in wartime espionage. One of the instructors was her beloved Shadowman from the earlier life. Although her conscious mind didn't understand why at the time, her heart knew that he was somehow important to her.

When she was ready, she was sent to occupied France to help run a safe house and do secret sabotage work. Saying farewell to her special instructor was a big emotional moment. She felt sad but also elated, without understanding why.

Then one day, after helping the Resistance in France for several months, she was caught.

I was waiting at a special place for a night-time parachute drop. It was out in the middle of nowhere, but the Germans came straight to me. They must have known I'd be there. I think we've been betrayed.

I'm going quietly in the hope that they'll loosen their grip on my arms. I'm looking for a chance to get away. It's important they don't torture me for information. I don't think I could hold out.

I have a suicide pill in my ring for exactly this situation. If I can't escape, I'll use that. But I must try to get away first.

*I suddenly yank myself away from them and run. I hear shots.
I keep running. My feet are lifting off the ground like a plane
taking off – I'm still running but it's in slow motion... oh...
I'm floating in the air.*

*I slow down and turn around. I can see my body lying on the
ground like a broken doll. They shot me. I'm dead.*

*Well, I can't be tortured now. They got no information out of
me. And I did it – I did what I meant to do with this life.*

There was a long silence during which I sensed she was still
engaged with these memories. Then she went on, with a
big sigh:

*I understand now. The angel has just been telling me a lot of
things about these past lives.*

*In the first one, my challenge was to get involved with
something serious. It was the next thing I had to do for my
soul to grow. I was good at being happy and carefree, but
I needed to experience something deeper than that. So the
chance came for me to join the secret group. It was ideal
because it was dangerous. I'd have to give it a serious level
of dedication. That's what the green ring stood for: it was to
remind me of my purpose in that life.*

*But I saw the secret society as just another way to have fun. I
expected to go on being treated like a lady of the court. When
that didn't happen, I gave up on it and went back to my
conventional beliefs. So that was the end of that.*

*After that I needed another life to complete what I hadn't
done in that one: to commit myself to a serious purpose.
Helping the French Resistance in World War II was perfect.
My ring with the suicide pill was like my green ring to the
power of ten.*

It's funny how that wartime life took me back to a large country house in France. I think it wasn't very far from where I lived in Renaissance times. Our different lives weave together in such strange ways. The angel told me that one day I'd meet my Shadowman again – and there'd be every chance that we'd be happy together at last.

I'm at peace with both of those lives now. I can let all that go now and move on.

Afterwards Gemma said she wished she could remember more about the secret things that Shadowman had told her. All she could recall was the pentagram that he'd drawn on the ground and his society's reverence for the goddess Venus.

The pentagram is such an ancient symbol that nobody knows where it really came from. In Sumeria 4,000 years ago it was a diagram of the astronomical orbit of Venus. Venus was important in the ancient world, standing for the benign feminine principle – the Queen of Heaven. Civilizations rose and fell, but the pentagram kept going through them all. In the Middle Ages it became a symbol of magical power. Gemma said when her Shadowman drew it, he was talking about the sun, the moon and the stars. So it may also have stood for astronomical knowledge that was taboo at the time.

Gemma was amazed at how she'd resolved her issues in a later lifetime. But this happens all the time. One life is too short for everything we need to do. The higher purposes of our soul path may span many lifetimes.

Whatever outer missions we may support in this world, we also have our own personal long-term aims. As we follow this secret inner purpose, the troubled events of one lifetime may turn out to be blessings in disguise. Looking back, we may see that they were the necessary stepping stones to the truly happy ending that we had always planned.

❖ ❖ ❖

18

CHANGING THE WORLD

It was a dance at the English royal court in 1348. The beautiful Countess of Salisbury was the belle of the ball. Knowing courtiers whispered that she was King Edward III's secret mistress. All eyes were on her and the king as they stepped through the formal dances together.

Then suddenly the countess's garter fell to the floor. The king swiftly picked it up, placed it on his own leg and said the now famous words, '*Honi soit qui mal y pense*' - ill to him who thinks ill of this.

The king had stepped in quickly because the colour of the lady's garter - green - signified that she was a priestess of the heretical old religion. Without that instant royal protection, she could have faced terrible consequences.

That was the beginning of the Order of the Garter, the first and still the most prestigious order of chivalry. In echoes of Arthur's Round Table, it began with 25 trusted knights chosen by the king to be his closest allies. The garter became the symbol of this order.

In those days, courtly people wore garments as coded signals about themselves, their status and accomplishments. In the mystical mindset of the time, this was never solely about physical achievements. In chivalry, the helmet, sword and spurs were all emblems of different degrees of initiation. Other symbols of personal prowess were shields, rings, medallions and seals. There were also items usually hidden - like the garter - which signified something that had to be kept secret.

The incident at court was the tiny tip of a hidden iceberg: secret magic in high society. Because esoteric knowledge was a means to empowerment, it was especially taboo for the poor. Vicious witchcraft trials served as a warning to keep the workers in their place. At higher levels of society, people could get away with more, though they still had to be careful. Their enemies would be glad of any chance to tattle tales to the priests.

Signs crop up throughout history of magic being secretly used by rulers while it was forbidden to the ordinary people. Roman emperors, German Nazis and even the Papacy have all been guilty of this.

The Nazis were obsessed with the occult and almost certainly used black magic. At the same time, they threw all other mystics, magicians, gypsies, astrologers and esotericists into their infamous concentration camps.

On the lighter side, in the seventeenth century Pope Urban VIII was a secret follower of the heresy of astrology. Suddenly afraid that an approaching eclipse might bring his death, he called on the heretical astrologer Tommaso Campanella to come to the Vatican and do his illegal rituals to ward off this danger.

When the Pope survived the eclipse, the astrologer took his chance to try introducing the Church to Hermetic philosophy, but didn't get very far.

One of Campanella's predictions sounds quite modern: he was convinced that the sun was coming closer to the Earth and that this would create a new golden age.

During Louis XIV's reign, the French courts were riddled with black magic. In 1679, a poisoning scandal erupted. Investigators looked into it and finally pointed the finger of blame at the priests. It turned out that they'd been helping a woman become the king's mistress by saying Masses to kill her rival and bewitch him in her favour.

Illicit uses of the Mass were nothing new. Complaints in 694 and again in the fifteenth century showed that priests had been using it for centuries to help kill people. They did this by holding a Death Mass for someone who was still alive. People's belief in the ritual gave it enough power to make it work.

Perhaps it was in reaction to all this high-level black magic that Freemasonry began as an esoteric society for stonemasons. Over time, men who had nothing to do with building also began to join up. In the eighteenth century, Freemasonry mushroomed. Many suspect that both the French and the American Revolutions were plotted within the walls of those lodges.

Past-life experiences of those times could be intense and significant. After the following dream, a friend of mine felt certain that in a former life she'd been involved with Freemasons in Revolutionary France:

> It was night. I was going with a few people to a secret meeting. This was during the French Revolution. On the way, I met two people who gave me secret signals. One of them used a special handshake. Another man was crouched on the pavement, holding his legs in a certain way. In the dream it was clear to me that this was how the Freemason secret signals had begun.

In pre-Revolutionary France an Egyptianized form of Freemasonry was very popular. The Lodge of the Nine Sisters was the most significant, with members like Robespierre, Marat, Benjamin Franklin and Christopher Wren – one of

Britain's most honoured architects. Inspired by the ideals of Freemasonry, he founded the Royal Society and redesigned London, with St Paul's cathedral his crowning achievement.

Key areas of Paris – the Louvre and the Avenue to the Champs Elysées – were also designed according to Masonic principles. In a fascinating talk on the subject, author Robert Bauval revealed that this was a deliberate replication of the ground plan of the ancient Egyptian city of Luxor.

In earlier times, on the other side of the Channel, Queen Elizabeth I regularly consulted her favourite magician John Dee about the best astrological dates for any enterprise. He almost certainly used occult rituals to help her plans to succeed.

Before Elizabeth came to the throne, Dee was imprisoned for several months for casting spells against her rival, the Catholic Queen Mary. Once Elizabeth was crowned, Dee was able to practise divination and *séances* openly and with official approval. Many thought that he was responsible for the sudden winds that came up to blow the Spanish Armada back, just when the Spaniards were poised to invade England and restore Papal control.

A lot of high-level magic was driven by the wish to create a better world. When the ancient Egyptian Hermetic Fragments surfaced during the Renaissance, it inspired people to think about using esoteric powers to transform society. During that time magic graduated from mainly personal use to a positive power for humanity in general.

This is what alchemy was really all about. The outside world thought alchemists were trying to physically change lead into gold, but that was just a symbol of what they called 'the Great Work', which was transforming both themselves and the world.

This was done in specific stages that could take many years. Each phase had its own colour. The word 'alchemy' comes from the Arabic *al-khame*, meaning 'the blackness'.

Black, or *nigredo*, was the first step – the death of the old self. The white, or *albedo*, stage was when the shattered self began to be put together again in a new way. The white hart was a symbol of this phase.

Rubedo, the red stage, was when the new self fully emerged. The emblem for this was the red lion – still the name of so many British pubs and streets today.

Alchemical gold was a much later development, which was only possible once the Red King had finally dissolved.

Past lives involved with alchemy will leave a strong impression on the psyche. If you feel affected by or drawn to any of its symbols, it may be because an old memory has been stirred. Sometimes simply focusing on the symbol will help to bring those experiences up into consciousness again.

When Kitty came for her regression, she felt strangely drawn to a small pestle and mortar that I have. It seemed likely to be a good memory aid for her, so she held it while I gave her the relaxation induction. Here's what she got:

> *Centuries of pounding grain – in Egypt, India, everywhere. Hundreds, thousands, millions of lives going into the crucible of the Earth and being pounded, pounded, life after life, their karma and experiences constantly being refined. The dross gets thrown away and the refined nature is kept. This takes a very long time. This is the main method, the big overriding thing that life on Earth does for people.*

> *Then there's a grain of refined corn in the mortar. The pestle is now turning, not pounding anymore. It turns round and round. The mortar fills with blood. It's thick and red. Lift the pestle now and then to check the consistency. Slowly the blood gets less thick.*

> *Little bits of silvery glitter start to appear. Keep on turning, but lightening it now and making it bigger. The mixture can*

now kind of float out of the mortar a bit, but not completely. It gets more and more glittery. Eventually it becomes like liquid silver glitter.

Turn and turn this as well, but lighter, more out of the crucible. It slowly expands and becomes even lighter. It turns into a golden cloud with tiny sparkles of glitter in it. I breathe that in.

Now I see myself as a medieval young man with a few others. We're being taught these things by an old alchemist. He's holding a pestle and mortar like this to demonstrate.

It's about the evolution and refinement of mankind. The silvery state is when people get more cosmic and can go beyond the Earth because their nature and consciousness have become more refined. The gold cloud is an even higher state. That's far in the future for the majority, but a few here and there have already achieved these transformations.

High-Society Magic

We tend to hear a lot about the antics of corrupt magicians and the shocking deeds of the dark side. But people seldom know about the positive esoteric work that also goes on at surprisingly high levels of society.

In her regression Yolande recalled a life in Edwardian England when she'd been involved in that kind of group.

She grew up in a wealthy mansion where her family regularly gave dinner parties for prominent people. At the age of about 13 she was initiated into one of those events:

I'm going out of my childhood and becoming an adult. I'm not very happy about it. There's a semi grown-up dress laid out for me. I'm being got ready to go to my first adult dinner party. There's going to be someone quite important there. I don't think I like him.

Now I'm sitting at the big dinner table with all the adults. I feel completely cowed. I'm trying so hard to remember to watch my manners that I don't say anything beyond the polite things.

This is a world where I have to just do the correct thing all the time. There's no room for any kind of what we'd call self-expression. As a young girl, I can't even come out with my opinions really.

I also suspect that there will be some kind of arranged marriage at some time. I'm very reluctant. And this is where it all starts – my first dinner party.

Later on, when she had been suitably married, Yolande's life took a more interesting turn: the woman who'd been her childhood nanny began to give her esoteric training:

There's a drawer in a dressing table that only I can get into. I keep the key with me all the time. Nobody must ever get into this drawer or find what's in it.

I go to that drawer and get out a book of secret occult knowledge. It's gorgeous. It's got illuminated borders. It's in Latin, but there are diagrams. It's very formal and ceremonial. It feels very old. There's so much to learn, it's quite daunting.

Paging through it now... there are illuminated letters... sigils... the Key of Solomon. It's all quite complicated. This isn't ordinary witchy sort of magic – this is to do with high magic. It's not for personal wishes, it's mediating on a specific esoteric level for the good of humanity.

Later, when she was ready, Yolande was initiated into the secret group.

There's a big network of these societies – very big. But they each work with a small number. This helps to maintain the secrecy.

AF: *What are their aims?*

Y: *We create astral doorways so that the masters from the esoteric planes can come through to us. This takes special training and preparation.*

There are different gateways for different reasons. Certain images and thoughts are used in specific ways. We use rituals that have been handed down through the tradition for hundreds of years. They've been repeated so often, by now they are real places on the astral plane. We reactivate those places every time we do the ritual. So we have stable meeting-places between the physical and the esoteric.

There is a vast purpose to all of this. Part of it is to do with how things are going to work out here on Earth – on the physical plane. That is all part of a greater invisible whole. So many things that happen in the world have esoteric significance because they are part of this plan working out.

There are also powerful beings who oppose the higher plan. The future of humanity is key. There is a sense that it is somehow being fought over at higher levels.

So, although the ancestors have knowledge of future possibilities, they need physical people to do the work here. Some of those people can be very powerful.

AF: *Do you mean magically powerful?*

Y: *I mean powerful in society. Titled people – even royalty somewhere along the line. They use their influence secretly, in good ways. A lot of the time they're trying to stop the effects of power misuse being so bad. They can also make it easier for certain things to take place.*

AF: *Can you recall anything that your group was focusing on at that time?*

Y: *There's a lot of discontent. Not just in my group – it goes beyond that. It's big. It runs through the whole network, and beyond in some way. Through other networks as well.*

AF: *What is this discontent about?*

Y: *The wrong king. Not an individual – in a general way. This goes beyond particular monarchs. It's been like this for a long time.*

It's after the war now [World War I, 1914–18]. So many people died. A lot of secret groups lost most of their people, so the ones who were left had to join together to make up the numbers – even join with people from different traditions. They had to learn to work with each other. And many of them didn't agree. These new arrangements weren't welcome. So it's all in flux at the moment.

There are other things going on as well, behind the scenes. The war shattered so much – much more than people realized. In the magical circles there's now a lot of division about the king – the power at the top. So there's a magical civil war going on. That's why he abdicated in the end.

In 1936 King Edward VIII abdicated because the British government was unwilling to accept the twice-divorced American socialite Mrs Wallis Simpson as his royal consort.

Before the war there were certain high-up people who worked with us. They could – they had been – working towards creating a much more – what's the word? – constructive, benign, supportive sort of world for people to live in. High-level decisions affect that more than people realize. So that purpose had been slowly going ahead.

Then the war scattered everything. It was intended to, we knew that. It had been foretold. But what dismayed many of us was the way in which all our attempts to rebuild were being scuppered by petty, silly issues.

So I decided I had to do what I could. This meant using whatever influence I had as well as I possibly could. My family had always been well connected; I knew some quite high-up people. So I did what I could within my social sphere to re-establish our esoteric influence. I gave the occasional dinner party, made useful introductions – that sort of thing.

I suppose all that early social training that I hated so much paid off in the end, because I knew exactly how to behave with these people and in these situations.

For the rest of that life, I just focused on doing whatever I could to keep my little boat within the occult movement steady and moving forward again and focusing on the future as constructively as possible. Many of our rituals became increasingly centred on these aims.

It was all quite long term. There were very few immediate or obvious results during those years. They weren't expected.

That was really the story of the rest of my life there – just continuing with my mission.

Which is pretty much what I'm still doing, I suppose. I understand more clearly now how long term this all is. And the need to be as patient about it as I eventually learned to be in that life.

Afterwards Yolande said that although it was unexpected, that memory made a lot of sense. It accounted for her strong interest in esoteric matters and also the sense she'd had all her life of some long-term mysterious mission.

'I had to be so formal and repressed in that life,' she said. 'I think this is why I'm so forthright now. I don't mince my words with anyone, whoever they are! It also explains why I love Edwardian fabrics and *décor*. So much is falling into place.'

The concept of the 'wrong king' intrigued us both. European folklore is rich with tales about a rightful king who is either in exile or too badly wounded to rule. Until he can be healed or restored, the people will live in a wasteland. The restoration of the true king means the healing of the land.

This idea may have arisen partly from traumatic memories of war and invasions. But clues in these tales point to roots that go much deeper than that. As we talked about it, the legends seemed to be more about how materialism and so-called rationality destroy our old mystical relationship with the Earth. This is what creates the wasteland. So the 'false king' means a false ideal.

The Holy Grail of this legend will stand for a truer understanding of life. Everyone who seeks the Grail of higher spiritual values is upholding the quest to restore the true king and heal the wasteland. This applies as much to people today as any other time.

'I've always had a sense that magic and politics go together more than people think,' said Yolande. 'It's to do with a higher purpose that's somehow behind history. A lot of things that happen are really because of battles between forces of light and darkness. I've always felt that. This memory has now shown me where that awareness came from.'

According to official history, it's only the famous people who change the world. The lives of so-called ordinary folk are assumed to have little influence on world events. And yet inventors, explorers, influential philosophers and political reformers all spring like daisies from grassroots beliefs and attitudes.

When the masses feel in their hearts that it's time for something, the right people emerge from that to implement the changes in a practical way. That happens automatically, even in times and places where rulers never bother to listen to the people. In more democratic times, the power of public outcry can change the course of history.

On top of that, the efforts of mystical individuals and esoteric societies to improve the world have immeasurable influence. Their work takes place primarily on the inner planes.

The world is really ruled by great hidden tides - not the people who think they're in charge. Those who know how to employ this can make a huge difference. They can affect the mass shifts in consciousness that later produce the visible movers and shakers of history.

Past lives doing this kind of work are usually like Yolande's - undramatic and unsung. But these lives are just as important as the famous ones - in some ways, maybe even more so.

The philosopher Ayn Rand said: 'Through the centuries there were people who took first steps down new roads armed with nothing but their own vision.'

Those people are the true pioneers, opening up new ways that others will follow later.

However unknown or obscure we may have been, the visions we pursued in our past lives have helped to make the world a better place. In recalling those lives, we can shake off the illusion of being ineffectual nobodies and reclaim a true form of empowerment - not the power to control others, but the power to make a positive difference.

19

HIDDEN POWERS

Where do our talents come from? Are skills randomly handed out? Is it just the luck of the draw that some people have genius-class abilities? Of course not.

'Genius is experience,' said Henry Ford. 'Some seem to think that it is a gift or talent, but it is the fruit of long experience in many lives.'

Past-life regressionist Arthur Bloxham said: 'If you can remember doing things well in a previous life, you can probably do them in this one too. I think all the great musicians and great artists of the past have been aware of having lived before, and that's why they become prodigies at a very early age.'

Our talents, skills and abilities are developed over the course of many lifetimes' training and practice. But not every kind of genius brings fame, or is recognized at all, even by the people involved. Many people have key abilities from their former lives that they ignore or undervalue. This is especially true of esoteric expertise.

There are many ways to trace these hidden talents. Our lives are full of clues about them. In his researches, Professor Ian Stevenson found that children often played at a favourite occupation from a former life. Think back to your childhood games – you might make some surprising discoveries.

Another sign of a past-life skill is that you will find it easy to do. If it feels as though you've been doing it for years, you probably have – in a former life. You may also feel attracted to practising that skill again – or something that closely resembles it, anyway.

Greta loved colour. She didn't think she was a particularly talented artist, but painting was her favourite activity. When she came for a regression, she found that in an ancient world she'd done colour-vibration healing. It was an exciting discovery and set her on a path of exploring different ways to use colour.

Hidden powers are sometimes heavily disguised. In her regression, Frankie went back to a life in ancient Egypt. She found that when she put her hand onto coded glyphs, the meaning would download into her mind.

The message she received was that she had a talent for breaking codes – and the chance might come for her to use it again in this life. The only inkling she'd had of this before the regression was her love of doing crosswords.

The Lady's Secret

Some past-life abilities are so powerful that they bring a high level of personal challenge and karmic responsibility with them. Inge discovered this when she regressed to a past life as the lady of a castle in medieval Scotland.

She was recovering from illness and spent a lot of time lying in bed with nothing to do. Little by little, she began to find herself drifting out of her body. She was amazed to discover that she could see what was going on in the rest of the castle and the country outside.

One day she saw her small son and his friends playing dangerously with some bows and arrows they'd found. Without thinking, she sent a messenger to stop them. After that, she started getting funny looks from people. How on earth could she have known that was going on? She realized she had to keep this ability very quiet or risk being branded as a witch.

The next unwelcome thing she saw was her husband's constant infidelities with the serving girls. She'd once been close to the castle priest and would normally have gone to him for advice and spiritual solace. But she was on her own with this.

To integrate these new developments she had to rethink all her old assumptions. As she did that, she slowly grew out of the rather insipid girl she'd once been.

A few years later, she saw far-off enemies coming to attack their castle. She had to decide whether to put herself in danger by revealing what she'd seen. Her stark choice was to either save herself or her people. She prayed for guidance, saying that if she had to sacrifice herself, she would.

The next day she knew exactly what to do. She told her husband that in a dream an angel had warned her that attackers were coming. That was acceptable to everyone – even the priest. Because this warning prepared them in time, the men of her castle won the battle.

Having to deal with these tricky issues entirely on her own made Inge strong. That strength became a permanent part of her inner self. Once she was aware of that past life, she understood much more about herself, her hidden powers and her future potential.

For hundreds of years, anyone admitting to the kind of ability Inge discovered would have been killed as a witch. By the twentieth century, this punishment had been downgraded from death to ridicule. This was still a severe penalty, however. It meant losing all personal credibility and could be the end of a good career. For many years it worked well as a tacit sanction to keep people in their place.

In the meantime, however, behind the Iron Curtain something else was stirring. Freed of their old religious constraints, Russians were researching the paranormal – partly out of curiosity and partly to develop powerful new weapons of the mind.

But in the spy-riddled world of the Cold War, nothing stayed secret for long. By the 1980s the CIA realized they had to catch up with this weird new form of warfare. So they started training psychic spies in the art of remote viewing. They called this project Operation Stargate.

After a few years, revelatory books began to come out about the military's new wing of esoteric training. Some of them were written by top remote viewers who'd left the services because their new skills brought better rewards in the private sector.

In 1995 Operation Stargate was officially closed down. The flow of books by remote viewers slowed to a trickle and now seems to have stopped altogether. I expect the whole project simply found a way to bury itself more deeply and plug all the old leaks.

Along the way, however, Operation Stargate gave us a great prize: we now know that remote viewing is real. The esoteric minority knew it all the time, of course. Despite the taboos and oppressions, throughout history certain people have always found ways to use the hidden powers of the mind. For some it comes naturally, as it did with Inge. Others are trained into it by secret societies.

Sending the Fetch

Holly went back to a life when, as a young man, she'd joined one of these sects in Elizabethan London. It was called something that was meant to sound vaguely alchemical, like the Black Hand. Similar little groups were mushrooming all over London at that time.

After some years of advancing within that society, the young man became the live-in personal secretary to one of their learned elders. Part of his job was copying out manuscripts of forbidden knowledge. He then had to deliver these copies to certain carefully selected people.

These were dangerous journeys. For protection, he drew on the training they'd given him, using a form of remote viewing known as sending the fetch.

'Fetch' is an ancient word for the astral double of a living person. It can also be a thought form created to do a special task. It works well as a messenger, both to send and to bring back information.

> **H:** *We can send out a tiny little version of ourselves to go and find things out. It flies off and it can go anywhere. Ordinary people don't see it.*

> **AF:** *When you do this, are you inside the little self and seeing through its eyes?*

> **H:** *I think some people can do that, but I can't. When it returns and gets back inside me, I know what it saw or found out. It takes practice, though. I'm still learning.*

> **AF:** *What sort of things have you found out in this way?*

> **H:** *It works best when I'm emotionally involved with what I want to find out. It isn't very motivated by abstract information. But that's fine, because I usually need to know if there is danger ahead. It's good at that.*

> *On one of my journeys to deliver a manuscript, my fetch showed me that an inn I planned to stay in overnight was full of danger for me. So I rode on further and found another place.*

Apart from these scrapes, it was a happy life and ended peacefully. Holly then recalled the afterlife world she'd gone to:

> It was so lovely. But I felt tired and fragile, as if after a long illness.

> I was left to wander round a lot. There was a beautiful garden there. I loved to sit in it and soak up all the beauty. It was like being in a healing bath.

> The guides in that place aren't at all judgemental. They're kind of like sports coaches analysing your performance, so you know what you need to work on. There's no sense of condemnation. I think we're the only ones who are ever hard on ourselves.

> They also help you to understand your lives. There are all kinds of amazing other layers to our experiences that we don't know about when we're here. So that's really fascinating.

> Dying isn't what people think it is either. It's quite a long process. It starts way before you leave the body. When I was lying there ill, but still in my body, I was seeing people from the other side. They were coming to prepare me to cross over.

> On the other side, I realized what wonderful gifts I'd been given in that life – the secrets I'd learned, the psychic powers I'd developed and the chance to do things to help make a better world – and I vowed to make the most of all that I'd been given in that life by honouring it in my future lives. This memory has come up now to remind me of that.

Remote viewing and using the fetch may sound like advanced magic, but actually we do these things all the time, unconsciously. The brain works like a receiver and transmitter and we are constantly sending out and picking up messages. This is why people sometimes pop into our minds just before they give us a call.

'What a coincidence! I was just thinking about you!' is something most of us have said at some time.

If someone keeps coming into your thoughts it's a sign that person is thinking of you. If you see them clearly in your mind's eye it's an even stronger indication that you are psychically connecting.

The next step is to literally see their astral double or fetch. Countless numbers of people have had this experience. The Society for Psychical Research received so many of these reports they had to give them their own section.

One famous example was when the eighteenth-century German writer Wolfgang von Goethe saw his friend Friedrich strolling along the road wearing the author's dressing gown. When he got home, he found Friedrich sitting in front of the fire. He'd been there the whole time – wearing Goethe's dressing gown because he'd been caught in the rain. Goethe had seen his astral double.

A firm believer in reincarnation, Goethe wrote, 'As long as you are not aware of the continual law of Die and Be Again, you are merely a vague guest on a dark Earth.'

The most common sightings of another's double usually happen at times of crisis. Author Colin Wilson said, 'So many people, from dukes to dustmen, have seen dying relatives at the moment of death that only the most dogmatic rationalist could dismiss it all as pure invention.'

And yet, despite all the evidence for their reality, our 'paranormal' mental powers are still somehow taboo. Perhaps it's because we don't trust ourselves, or each other, to exercise them properly. This leaves the field open to the unscrupulous to use these skills for their own ends, while everyone else hesitates in the face of these fears.

It's been said that we only use 10 per cent of our brains. It looks as though we're now poised on the brink of extending that and developing our latent inner powers. Like any resource, this has the potential for both good and ill, but I'm convinced the positive will outweigh the negative and will win in the end.

In Eddie's regression he got to the heart of this issue:

I'm floating high above a snowy medieval town. I can see myself in one of the houses. I'm a boy of about 12 or 14. I have books. I'm excited about all the things I'm learning. I try to share this with my mother, but she's too busy with the baby and hanging out washing in the kitchen.

I see myself grow up. I study a lot and join a secret society. I'm learning so much, it's wonderful. But we are persecuted. The people in charge don't want us to have this knowledge. It's too empowering. I see my comrades killed.

But then I see their spirits rise up out of their bodies, laughing, with their books of knowledge held to their hearts.

A white-robed angel is with me. He lets me know that this knowledge – these abilities – were given to the human race by God. It will continue. It will be developed. It will not be quenched.

Edgar Cayce said that with a bit of practice, it was easy to foster past-life talents again. He said that the large numbers of Atlanteans who would reincarnate during the twentieth century would have a lot of valuable knowledge to share – including the latent powers of the mind. They would also bring with them a keen awareness of the karmic consequences of abusing that knowledge. Even if the Atlantean memories remained subliminal for those who reincarnated from that time, their subtle influence would do much to safeguard the future of human development.

Yes, fire can be destructive. Yes, criminals can abuse it. But the benefits fire brings offset its dangers so much that no sane person would dream of trying to ban its use. As we reclaim our forgotten skills and hidden powers, one day we may look back and see them as we now see fire: as a sign of evolution and an indispensable part of civilized life.

20

SECRETS OF THE KNIGHTS TEMPLAR

Many people are aware of their past-life connections with clandestine societies, but accessing the secrets they once knew is not always so easy. It sometimes feels as though a protective psychic ring has been put around that information. The societies themselves may have done that for their own protection, but the strong thought forms they created can carry on doing that job long after the group has dispersed.

Our personal vows of secrecy can be just as potent. They had to be deeply engraved on the psyche, because the dangers were so real. As a result, even lifetimes later, they are still active. Because of this, when we reach a certain point along the path of exploration, our own past selves may step forward like sentries and block us from going any further.

In my experience, one of the most guarded organizations was the Knights Templar. Even people whose lives are full of hints about past-life connections to the Templars often have problems accessing the actual memories of this organization.

Right from the start, the Templars had a secret purpose that has never been fully revealed. Early in the twelfth century, French nobleman Hugues de Payens picked eight trusted knights from his own family and announced that the mission of this little band was to protect pilgrims on journeys to the Holy Land. There's little evidence they ever did this, though.

What they actually did was go to Jerusalem on an undisclosed assignment of their own. King Baldwin II of Jerusalem let them set up their headquarters in the Al Aqsa Mosque on Temple Mount. This was also the site of the fabled Temple of Solomon – which was their true interest. They called themselves the Knights of the Temple of King Solomon, which was later shortened to Knights Templar.

While there, they undertook underground excavations of the ancient Temple. Many suspect they found a great treasure there – maybe even the fabled Ark of the Covenant. What they did find is still a mystery. But when they returned to France, they rapidly became one of the most powerful and wealthy organizations in Europe. They set up a banking system, lent money to kings, and even had some kind of power over the Pope, because for many years they were exempt from Papal rule.

Although we may never know what physical treasure the Knights Templar found, there are clear signs that they brought back a wealth of Middle Eastern esoteric knowledge – which was dangerously taboo in Christian Europe, of course.

Much of it probably came from the educated Arab men the knights employed as translators, interpreters and secretaries. They also formed a close association with the Druse – a spiritual sect that is still operational in Lebanon.

Another group they became involved with was the Hashishim. The word 'assassin' comes from this name. These men used the drug hashish in rituals to prepare themselves for their sacred task of contract killing. For reasons that are still mysterious, they donated money to the Templars through most of the twelfth century.

Exposure to these different views of life made a huge impact on the knights. In those days in the Middle East there was no division between science and spirituality. Mathematics, alchemy, astrology and magic all skipped merrily along together.

In addition, because Islam forbids the depiction of people or animals in religious art, complex abstract design became the high art of Moslem spirituality. Sacred geometry was a natural outcome of this practice. It was a concept that the Templars embraced wholeheartedly.

One of my clients recalled a life when he signed up with the Templars, went out to the Middle East with them – and never came back. Instead he married and settled down in a beautiful big house, happily surrounded by his wife's huge family. The lifestyle was so preferable to what he'd known in Europe that he refused to return. He was probably one of many who 'went native' and defected.

Those who did return set to work building their great Notre Dame cathedrals of Paris, Chartres, Reims and Amiens. They encoded the design and carvings of these grand structures with the secret principles of sacred geometry, astrological references and many other mysteries.

Then, almost a century after they'd begun, the Templars were suddenly struck down. On Friday 13 October 1307, Templars throughout France were arrested in dawn raids. They were accused of bizarre heresies and many of them were viciously tortured and killed.

I know a few people who show signs of having had Templar past lives – such as a deep fascination with their history, and sympathy for their cause – but they have so far not accessed those lives. Perhaps it's not the right time for them to recall what could have been horrific experiences.

Our psyche will always protect us from anything that might be harmful to us. So, for many people, direct memories of that dark patch in Templar history remain veiled.

The ones who got away scattered, many fleeing to England and Scotland. When British place names include the word 'Temple' it's a sign of old Templar settlements in the area.

In his regression, Axel recalled being one of the Templars who managed to escape to England. The group he was with landed in Bristol and settled nearby. He said he always felt that the upper echelons of the Templars had secret knowledge that they didn't share with the rank and file.

Even in those days, Glastonbury was a place of spiritual pilgrimage. In that life Axel yearned to go there, but never made it.

In his next incarnation, he became a scholarly monk. He was still seeking knowledge – and still haunted by a sense of secrets beyond his reach because they were only for the élite.

He said that in his current life he had learned that real wisdom came from the inner journey. This understanding finally opened up the way to Glastonbury for him. He has now realized that he'd been looking for his Grail in the wrong places. When he found it within himself, the outer symbol of it could then come into his life.

The Templars who moved to Britain might have inspired and even founded organizations like the Freemasons and Rosicrucians. It's probably no coincidence that some key Freemason symbology refers to the Temple of Solomon. However, instead of building physical churches as the Templars did, Freemasons think of the Temple of Solomon as an inner ideal. With the aid of building symbology such as the square and compasses, they intend to create this temple within themselves as they advance through the degrees. Does this mean the Templars started again as Freemasons?

Like so much else about these mysterious knights, solid facts about this remain elusive.

Yet facts are not the only path to truth. There are other ways to get to the heart of the Templars. Just a few years after they began, fresh stories about Arthurian knights and the quest for the Holy Grail began to circulate and it looks as though the Templars were linked to the revival of these ancient legends.

The Templars themselves had a council of the round table, at which each knight was expected to carry his sword. Their churches were also round. The knights upheld a high code of chivalry. Their courage in battle was legendary. Mysticism and magic surrounded them. It does seem that the Grail tales that came out during their time may be the best expression we have of Templar philosophy.

A symbolic approach also works well in accessing Templar past lives. One day, I was surprised to become aware that a Templar was with my client like a benign spirit guide.

When I told her what I'd seen, she said she'd first become aware of him on the flight over from New Zealand. She knew that he was there to help her in a good way.

Her next stop was the south of France, where she felt she was going to reconnect with past-life issues in some way. She knew her Templar guide was part of that – and he'd somehow see her through whatever she needed to find out.

When she came for a regression, Jill also discovered that her Templar past was a source of strength in her current life. This is what first came up for her:

> *I'm getting a strong sense of what I was like when I was one of the Knights Templar. I had a really tough-minded devotion to the cause, whatever the discomforts or sacrifices.*

I can see now that clues about this life have been popping up now and then, but I've been ignoring them.

This is coming up now to remind me that the inner strength I had in that life is still a part of me now. When I need it, I can call on it.

There's a Templar standing in front of me. He's very serious. He's presenting me with a sword. It's not for killing anyone, it's a symbol of inner strength. I take it from him and bow. When I look up, he's gone.

In the second part of her regression, Jill received this message about the Templars and their role in the world today:

A wizard with a long white beard leads me into the main hall of a castle. There are flags hanging on the walls. They have strange symbols on them that seem somehow alive and powerful.

Now I see figures of Templar knights standing against the walls in some kind of suspended animation. The wizard tells me that this court is the centre of a belief system. These figures are ideas, not people.

The knights are latent powers. When the time is right – when it's necessary – they are awakened and released into the world. The timing is important.

He says many have been released in recent years. This is why new ideas and concepts are spreading. But the dark side does the same sort of thing. The 'knights' have to fight for the hearts and minds of the people.

The final result will be what the people have chosen. The wizard said because of this he was sure that in the end the good side would win.

ACCESSING YOUR TEMPLAR PAST LIVES

Did you have a past-life connection with the Knights Templar? All kinds of clues may point to this possibility. Feeling drawn to finding out more about them is one of the strongest signs. Trepidation about it is another big clue.

If you delve into their history, notice your reactions to the different bits of information as you go along. Our feelings are messengers, coming directly from the deeper self. If we heed them, they can tell us secrets and enrich our lives in so many ways.

When it's time to unearth this past-life connection, Templar knights may begin to come into your dreams. They might visit you in your meditations or visualizations. Pictures or references to them could start coming to your attention.

As with any other past life, if you make a note of these signs and synchronicities, a pattern will start to emerge.

What to do about it then? Some Templar past lives may contain secrets that aren't yet ready to be told. Others may still be too traumatic to recall. The best way forward may be to deal with Templar memories at the symbolic level.

You could ask for insights in your dreams or meditations, remembering to call on your guardian angels and spirit guides for help and protection. Perhaps call up a benign and positive knight to be your guide through this strange territory.

Remember that the pieces of your bigger picture will fall into place at just the right moment for you.

21

THE RETURN JOURNEY

All life has natural cycles and rhythms. We can see it in the stately dance of night and day, winter and summer. Flowers open and close, tides go in and out – and our lifetimes have their cycles as well.

In one life, we may join a secret society and become intensely involved in its work to improve the world. That may go on for more than one incarnation, but sooner or later we need a break. When that time comes, the old doors will start to close and a new direction will open up.

This change doesn't have to be abrupt. As Carson found in her regression, letting go of the excitements of secret societies may be a journey in itself.

She booked a session because she'd been offered a great job in local government and wanted to find out why she felt so ill at ease about it.

Her memory began with walking in a beautiful garden. She said the house looked Chinese. She was a young girl of about 16, the daughter in that home. She was wearing colourful but formal clothes. It seemed that she always had to have an elaborate hairstyle and full make-up.

As she went back to the house, she had a feeling of foreboding. As soon as she was inside, a servant scurried up to her saying her aunt wanted to see her in the courtyard.

I go and join her there. We're sitting at a stone table. I can tell from her face that something is wrong. I'm feeling nervous. The servant brings us a tray of tea. My aunt pours us a cup each before she starts talking.

Then she tells me my father has had to go away suddenly – a business trip to somewhere very far away. We don't know when he'll be back.

AF: *What sort of business is he in?*

C: *Materials. Textiles. Mainly silk, I think. Now she's saying the business trip is just a cover story. The real reason he's gone is because trouble has suddenly flared up.*

It's because he's secretly against the Emperor and something's been found out, so he must get out of the way for a while. She says we'll all have to be very careful now. The Emperor's spies are everywhere these days.

AF: *Have you any idea what time period this is in?*

C: *I get the number 868. But I don't know what that means.*

(A few days later)

C: *It's night. I haven't been able to sleep. I can hear angry voices. I've crept out of my room so I can secretly listen to them.*

(Whispering) It's my aunt and my mother. They're having a big row. It's about the trouble my father is in. My aunt is blaming some secret group he belongs to. She says he was a fool to trust people like that – people who do black magic.

I've heard enough. I'm going back to my room before they find me. My own father belongs to a secret magical society! I didn't know that.

I feel so excited. I knew they existed. Everyone does. Those groups have strong magic. People say they're using it to bring down the corrupt Emperor. And my father is part of that! Maybe I can join them. I've always wanted to do something like that.

(The memory moved ahead to the next event.)

The monk has come to visit us. He's not really a monk, people just call him that. They say he once belonged to a secret order that taught him some powerful magic. He's obviously part of my father's secret society. This is my chance: I'm going to talk to him.

I go and sit with him. I ask him if occult groups really exist. He laughs but doesn't answer. I say if there are any groups like that, I want to join one. He looks at me with raised eyebrows.

Oh no, here comes my aunt. She doesn't look very happy. She orders me to go to my room. I have to go. I feel so embarrassed.

A bit later she comes to my room, very angry with me. She heard everything I said to the monk. She tells me he's really a government spy, and the Emperor's people all use black magic. Oh... I didn't know that.

She says I'm too young and naïve for this. Those people would use me like a dishrag if I got involved with them, so she told the monk that I was just playing a silly game. I feel so stupid now.

(A few years later)

The danger seems to have passed. My father is home again. I'm walking in the garden with him. He's telling me that *he's managed to get a place for me in the house of a high-up official. Their houses are like government departments. My father says I'll learn about the ways of the Emperor while I'm there, but I'll have to be careful because of his past. Even though things have gone quiet, they still suspect him of being against the Emperor. He says the minister's people will try to trip me up because they want to get at him.*

I don't want to work for the Emperor's people, but my father says while I'm there I'll be able to do some spying for him. So I'm happy with that. We bow to each other. That means an agreement.

Carson's work in the large house turned out to be mostly ceremonial. Her main task was to greet visitors and provide them with tea and polite conversation while they waited to see other people. It gave her the ideal opportunity to spy for her father, but it was difficult to get messages to him. She hardly ever had time off to go home, she couldn't trust the messengers, and when her father came to visit her, they were never left alone.

Eventually they hatched a plot: she'd get information to him through her poems. They'd look like innocent little pieces about nature, but every element in them would be a code for something else. It seemed foolproof – but she still had a feeling that she was being watched.

Then one day she had a shock:

I was walking in the big gardens here. They are always tidy and well kept, but I saw the dead body of a fox right in the middle of the path. It was half rotten and maggoty – horrible! The gardeners would remove any dead thing long before it got into that state, so I knew it was put there on purpose.

If I'd mentioned a dead animal in one of my coded poems it would have been a big warning to stop everything because of hidden danger. Especially a fox. I think they're using my own code to let me know that they're on to me.

This is very frightening. I think I'm in big danger. And if I am, my family is too.

(Pause)

The next time my father came, we gave the guards the slip for once and went for a walk. I told him what had happened. He said I must stop the poems and all spying work from now on. I must also keep away from the occult things that went on around there.

I went to ask a herbal woman what sort of omen a dead fox could be. I didn't tell her anything about my life. She said it meant I'd be in terrible danger if I carried on down the path I was on. So I stopped everything after that. I even had to stop listening to gossip about magicians. I told people that I wasn't interested in that stuff anymore. It was so difficult to do that. I really, really missed it.

(A few years later)

I'm married now. My family sent me to do that work in the hope that I'd marry one of the high-up officials. So that worked out.

I'm living with my husband right out in the country. We have a big house and a lot of land. We're in charge of this area. My husband has to oversee the farmers. He's supposed to show them the best ways to manage the land. We help them as much as we can.

The Emperor's minister comes to see us now and then. We always fill up his cart with vegetables and things, so he goes away happy. It's so funny to see him in all his finery and dignity coming down the muddy track in his creaky, wobbly cart.

AF: *How do you feel about this way of life?*

C: *At first I wasn't happy to be stuck out here, so out of the loop of everything. But my father says it's people like us who will bring the changes we want.*

AF: *How will you do that?*

C: *We can use the land to become rich and strong. If we join with others who think like us, we'll control bigger and bigger areas. That will give our network a lot of power.*

In time, Carson found something else that more than made up for leaving behind the world of intrigue:

*There's an old couple here. They're part of the household...
and they've turned out to have a lot of secret wisdom. They've
started to teach me things.*

*They say everything has a god or a spirit. Not just the things
we already know about – the spirits of natural things like
hills and trees and the wind, or even our household gods –
but other things as well, that you wouldn't expect: towns,
villages, groups of people, events, situations – everything,
really. When you know that, you can connect with the spirit
of anything. Find out what it intends. Maybe ask it favours
if it's friendly enough. Knowing this opened up an exciting
new world for me.*

*They also taught me how to spot the special clues that will tell
you about the real inner nature of something. I practised that
a lot and learned how to see beneath surface appearances. I
began to be able to see through people.*

*I remember a ragged man once came to the door. He was
selling trinkets. A bit of red cloth was peeping out of his shoe.
My inner senses told me it meant he was dangerous.*

*I bought a small thing and sent him on his way. Then I shut
down all his inner pathways to coming back here. Later on I
heard that he had once killed someone.*

*The old couple changed my life. I finally stopped hankering
after political intrigue or secret magic societies. This way was
so much better.*

*Images from that life are getting misty now. Moving away...
getting smaller... vanishing into the distance... gone.*

'This must be why the idea of working for the government
was bothering me so much,' Carson said afterwards. 'It was
like going back to something dangerous – something I'd had
to leave behind. I can see where that fear came from now. I
feel better about taking this job.'

A few weeks later she sent me this e-mail:

*I've been doing some research. Before I came to you, I
knew absolutely nothing about Chinese history and when
you asked me when that life took place, the number 868
just came to me from nowhere. Out of curiosity, I decided
to look up what China was like in that year.*

*The year 868 was during the T'ang dynasty. It was a great
time. There was a lot of prosperity. The arts were flourishing.
Poetry was very fashionable. Remember how I wrote little
poems in that life? Turns out I was right on trend!*

*There was also masses of political unrest. So that fits as
well, with all the anti-Emperor stuff that was going on in
my family.*

*Around then the Imperial government had a bright idea
about how to make the land more productive. They
started handing out pieces of property to wealthy families
for them to manage.*

They guessed those families would try to build up their power by getting more land for themselves, so they thought up all kinds of schemes to try and stop that happening. But none of it worked. These new landlords made sure they got the loyalty of the local people. And that's exactly what we did. We made a big point of being nice to all the people who worked for us and lived round there.

Exactly like my family, everyone was busy trying to get more property through marriage. So after a while a powerful landed élite emerged. In the end they chucked out the Emperor, which they'd been aiming to do all the time – just as my father had predicted.

I was absolutely amazed when I found all that out. The history of that time describes my life exactly as I got it in the regression.

Our incarnational journey often follows specific themes that we want to study. To do that, we'll take lives that will show us every aspect of the subject we're delving into, including its opposite or lack.

We may have chosen experiences in secret societies to explore a wide variety of themes – the most common being initiations, secrecy and hidden wisdom. This personal tour of discovery can lead us into many different situations, immersing us in all kinds of clandestine clubs and underground associations.

Those times would have been highly educational. Esoteric groups tend to provide intense experiences and a steep learning curve that moves people quickly along the path of personal growth. So these lives may have been tough, but on looking back, for most people they were among their best and most significant.

I also get the impression that many who went that route are beginning to feel that it's now time to move beyond the undercover ways that were so necessary in the Piscean Age. Having sloughed off the negative effects of that era, they can move forward, knowing that the valuable knowledge they gained in those lives will always be part of them.

As we hopefully move towards more relaxed and open times, we'll be able to share openly the things that we once had to learn in secret. Together we'll be able to build a brighter new world because of the wisdom that we attained through all those hard-won experiences.

YOUR PAST-LIFE MEMORIES OF SECRET SOCIETIES

Remember, this visualization will introduce you to your past-life memories in a safe and gentle way. You'll be able to view scenes from your past lives as a detached observer, without needing to relive any of the experiences. Whenever you wish, you can stop the exercise simply by opening your eyes. For extra reassurance, ask your guardian angel or spirit guide to be with you.

Repeat this exercise whenever it feels right. At first you may get only brief glimpses of your memories, but with practice you'll gather a lot of information about your past lives. As you go along, you'll begin to see the bigger picture of your soul's reincarnational journey. This will help you to understand much more about your current life and how it fits into your higher purpose.

- ◎ *Preparation:* Sit or lie somewhere where you can be quiet and undisturbed.

- *Relaxation:* Scrunch up and expand all your muscles – especially your face, hands, arms and shoulders. Then let all your muscles soften and relax.

- *Focus:* Become aware of everything that's underneath you. Sense how comfortable, firm and supportive it is.

- *Centre yourself:* Gaze steadily at a candle or a crystal until you want to close your eyes.

- *Clear your mind:* Breathe slowly and deeply, right down to your stomach. Listen to the sound of your breath.

- *Approach the gateway:* Imagine that you're lighting a candle in a dark room. You'll see your guide in a hooded cloak waiting for you. They will show you to a secret door behind a tapestry.

- *The doorway:* You follow your guide through this doorway and go down some steps to a long and well-built underground passage. In this passage you'll see clues about your different past-life times and places.

- *The reminders:* Your guide leads you to a special room. A fire is blazing merrily in the grate. Let its warmth soothe and comfort you. You look around, noticing many reminders of the old days.

- *Observe and explore:* Choose a picture that may be in a book or on the wall and look deeply into it. As you gaze into it, scenes from your past lives in secret societies will unfold.

- *Return:* When you feel ready to leave, thank your guide and return smoothly and gently to the present.

PART IV
MAGICIANS

'The will has far greater power than we realize.
Magic is learning how to use that power.'
Colin Wilson

INTRODUCTION

What is a magician? The word comes from the Latin and Greek *magia*, meaning the occult knowledge and practices of the Persian *magi*. Since then, the term has expanded to include vastly more than that.

We now think of magicians, wizards or witches – of either gender – as people with supernatural power. This power comes from their connection with other levels of reality and their knowledge about those realms.

The magician knows from direct experience that all reality, including the physical world, is non-ordinary. It has mysterious rules, hidden from most people, which the magician has learned and knows how to use.

One of those keys is the knowledge that everything is linked and bound together as if in a giant web. This is the foundation of all esoteric ritual.

Because everything is connected, nothing that happens is random or insignificant. Knowing this makes it easy to understand signs and omens. Carl Jung called these meaningful coincidences 'synchronicity'.

In this unified reality, all kinds of mysterious influences surge under the surface like ocean currents. Mostly unaware of them, nations and individuals ebb and flow with these tides. What people call magic is the knowledge of how to work with these influences, using symbols, rituals, words, images and intent.

Magicians are also those who have graduated from their apprenticeship and can work proactively on their own. Even when they're involved with esoteric groups, they don't really need them. This independence is both their strength and their Achilles heel. Shamans serve their tribe, priests and priestesses serve a religion, but nobody knows what a magician serves. This makes people wary of them. Down the centuries, self-sufficient female magicians have been especially hated and often persecuted as witches.

One of the reasons for this fear is that the magician is a psychological archetype. Everyone has their own inner magician. Most people are scared of this aspect of themselves, however. They keep it buried in the unconscious and project their qualms about it onto others.

In the words of Nikolai Tolstoy, 'The centuries come and go, literary fashions pass, but the magician reappears before us: shifting his shape and changing his name, now mocking, now awe-inspiring. Trickster, illusionist, philosopher and sorcerer, he represents an archetype to which the race turns for guidance and protection.'

These conflicting views also come from fears of the dark potential of magical power. Rumours about the shenanigans of sorcerors such as Grigori Rasputin, Dr Faust or Aleister Crowley feed into those concerns. In our deepest heart we may wonder whether, if we had that much power, we could really be sure we'd use it well.

That is one of the key reasons ethical people – the vast majority – hold back from claiming their inner power.

Unfortunately, this leaves the field free for the feckless minority to dominate it.

How can we change that? By believing in the positive side of magicianship, both within ourselves and in others. One way to do that is by looking at past-life memories of the times we used magic. Those lives are seldom as bad as we expect and it's often a huge relief to discover that. We can also own our inner magician and help to change the world by working with the issue at archetypal levels.

Our culture's most dominant prototype defines the world we live in. For a long time now, the model of the Warrior has ruled us. In that mindset, life is about overcoming mainly physical obstacles. Warriors deal with problems by eliminating them. They are dragons to be slayed, whether by words, guns or sabres of light. This attitude has created a male-centric, warlike world.

But, as writer Celeste Adams says, 'A shift is occurring. The Magician is emerging as an archetype that may play a central role in the Third Millennium. It will replace the Warrior as our culture's most important figure.'

This change is coming from within us. Folklore, art, films and stories are all good mirrors to these transformations of the mass consciousness. The popular film *Avatar* was a communal rite of passage away from the Warrior model to a more peaceful, magical way of life.

Over the last century, the image of the magician has been steadily moving towards the positive. In the oldest Marseilles Tarot cards, the Magician is little more than a conjurer. But the later Rider–Waite pack depicts him as a figure of wisdom and enlightenment.

For the first half of the twentieth century, more optimistic views about magic were quietly gathering pace under the surface. Then, in 1951, came a watershed moment: bowing to pressure from the Spiritualist churches, the British government finally repealed the ancient English law against witchcraft.

In 1954, Gerald Gardner published *Witchcraft Today*. This book revolutionized public opinion about magic. The icon of the wicked witch stirring up a cauldron of trouble morphed into a devout keeper of pagan traditions. Wicca came into the open as a benign force for good. Because of this new definition, it now attracts a majority of positive practitioners.

In more recent years, giant figures of benevolent magic like Gandalf and Professor Dumbledore have been striding through the mass psyche, sweeping away old prejudices. They may have begun as fiction, but I believe that with the help of people like you, these symbols have the potential to transform our culture in positive ways that we haven't yet begun to imagine.

22

THE SWORD IN
THE STONE

Arthurian legends aren't about the worldly power of kings – they are about the spiritual path. The stories are full of universal symbolic meanings that apply to everyone's personal journey.

Norse legend has a similar tale: the god Odin embedded a sword into a special tree and the hero Sigmund was the only one who could draw it out.

The British version of this archetypal story opens with the birth of Arthur as the rightful heir to the throne. Merlin the magician knew that great dangers lay in wait for the child. He therefore made sure that the boy would grow up hidden away where no one would know his true identity. For added protection, Arthur would be encouraged to forget who he really was.

This is about the human condition. In the realms outside physical incarnation, our consciousness is unbound. We know who we are, where we've been and where we're going. This is what kingship stands for in the legends. When we incarnate, that awareness becomes unconscious. We grow up like Arthur did, forgetting our real nature. We nevertheless remain true heirs to the throne – in other words, this condition is only temporary. It's also not a mistake. Merlin, the symbol of wisdom, arranged it this way to keep us safe.

Merlin knew that a time would come when Arthur would have to claim his rightful heritage. This means that sooner or later – maybe after many lifetimes – every one of us will blossom into greater awareness. It's important that this happens at the right time and only when we're truly ready for it.

To make sure of that, Merlin set up a test: he embedded a sword in a stone. On the stone he wrote in gold letters: 'Whosoever pulls this sword from this stone is the true heir and rightful king.'

The stone represents the world of matter. The sword stands for the latent powers of the mind that we all have within us – what people usually call magic.

The sword in the stone represents circumstances that come to us that can only be solved by using our innate inner powers. When we magically draw the sword from the stone, it's the first step towards reclaiming our true heritage.

The story says that before Arthur comes, many try to draw the sword from the stone and fail. They symbolize the chances we didn't take – the times when we weren't ready to access our latent powers.

Then Arthur comes along. This means we're ready. It's time to do this. He draws the sword from the stone: we have become aware of our inner powers. He becomes king: there's no turning back.

This test can come to us in many different ways. A tough crisis is the most common. If we can find more obvious solutions, we won't bother to use our inner powers. It's only when our backs are truly against the wall that we will draw the sword from the stone. This can happen in all kinds of strange ways – and usually when we least expect it.

The Stalled Car

A visitor from Australia, Lily, told me how her pilgrimage to Avalon had really begun with a strange incident that had happened years before:

> I was driving a long way into the outback to spend some time with an old friend who'd moved out there. It was a long and hot journey. I'd packed some refreshments, so when I saw a place where I could park under a shady tree I stopped there.
>
> But when I tried to get going again, the car wouldn't start. I didn't have a mobile phone in those days, so I was stranded in the middle of nowhere. I hadn't seen another car for hours. I started to feel panicky.
>
> Then I had the strangest experience. At that time I wasn't into any kind of otherworldly stuff. There's no way I would have thought up anything like this. It was as if something in me just took over the whole situation.
>
> I suddenly felt completely calm. I opened the car bonnet and looked at the engine. Now I still know absolutely nothing about how cars work, but I suddenly felt that I knew exactly what I was doing. I found two loose wires and tied them together. When I tried the car again, it started! And it went fine, all the way to my friend's house. I was so relieved when I got there.
>
> I told my friend all about it and to my surprise, she believed me. We spent the evening sitting on the porch, looking at the stars and talking about all the spooky things we could remember. That evening is one of my favourite memories now.

Lily came for a regression to see if she could find out any more about that strange event. A vivid memory soon surfaced. She was a young man living in a poor community. As the memory unfolded, she became sure this was in the hills of Kentucky in the 1940s. She recalled:

I had a real old banger of a car. It was one step away from the scrapyard, but it was all I could afford. I had to know how to fix it, so I learned all about how cars worked.

Pretty soon I was helping other people round there fix their old cars as well. None of us could afford proper garage repairs – we had to make do and mend with everything – so I helped out where I could, and didn't charge anything for it. If they could do me a favour some other time, that would be fine, but it wasn't important. I was just glad to help out.

In the second part of the regression, I directed Lily to go to a beautiful place where she could connect with a spirit guide about this. She found herself in the Australian outback, far from anywhere. It was twilight. A short distance away, a small group of Aborigines was gathered round a campfire. They were dressed and painted for a special ceremony. Lily said she loved the sound of their soft chanting. She felt she should keep her distance and watch from afar.

Presently, a great spirit of blue and white light came through from the higher realms. It floated above the campfire, giving blessings to the little group. Then it noticed Lily. It sent a beam of soft light that surrounded her. She said it felt wonderful – warm and loving.

The light being let her know that her generosity to others in the Kentucky life had brought her a lot of good karma. That was why when she was stranded, her past-life knowledge of cars had come to her rescue.

This incident was also her destined wake-up call. It had been meant to happen to put her onto her spiritual path.

The final message she received was that she was making good progress and the spirits were pleased with her.

Afterwards Lily mused:

> It's funny, but even though I've never been there,
> I've always felt kind of sentimental about Kentucky.
> Whenever it's mentioned I feel a little pang. Now I
> know why.
>
> I have the feeling that connecting with that past life was
> meant to be my gateway. From now on, I'll be able to
> remember other past lives and other knowledge I once had.
> When I got that car started again, it was really the start
> of a completely new phase in my life.

The Green Cloak

Another crisis that can push people into discovering their inner powers is psychic attack. Bella related the following experience:

> I'd recently dumped a bloke because I felt he was trying
> to take over my life. He had rather grand ideas about
> himself. It was quite early in the relationship, so I thought
> it would be enough to just give him the usual polite lines
> – you know the kind of thing – and he seemed to accept it
> without any problem.
>
> About a week later, I started getting more and more
> depressed. I kept thinking how worthless I was, and that
> I'd be better off dead. It was really heavy stuff. I also
> started having little accidents with knives. That was what
> woke me up.
>
> I suddenly remembered something I'd read about how
> psychic attack worked and I realized that was it – it

was probably the bloke I'd ditched sending me all those terrible thoughts.

I made up my mind that he wasn't going to do this to me, and I did all the psychic protection things I'd ever read about: surrounded myself and my home with protective blue light, practised affirmations, focused only on positive things...

I kept that up for a week or two, but I had the impression that it worked almost immediately. I think the strongest magic was simply realizing what was happening and deciding to stop it.

During that time I had an amazing dream. In it, I found a wonderful green cloak. It was embroidered in gold with magical symbols and had a big mandala on the back. It also had a large hood in looser, softer material.

I loved it and wanted it, but thought it probably cost hundreds of pounds. I asked a man who was standing there how much it was. He said £25. I was delighted and said I'd have it.

When I put the cloak on, I was surprised to see blood on my arms. I looked in the mirror and saw that my face was bruised, especially around one eye. I realized I'd been attacked, yet I had no memory of it.

I was determined to find out what had happened. Still wearing the cloak, I marched off with great determination to have it out with someone. That was the end of the dream.

The weirdest thing of all was when I woke up next morning and looked in the mirror, I had blood in one eye. I have no idea how that could have happened. It was obviously connected with the dream and the telepathic harassment I was going through.

The last thing I remember in the dream was striding off to confront someone. Maybe I had some kind of dust-up with that bloke on the astral plane.

It was such a strange experience, but in the end it did me no real harm. In fact I think it strengthened me. Now I know how psychic attacks work and how to deal with them. As the dream showed, it was a small price to pay for getting a wonderful magical cloak.

By the time she felt ready to find out more about this, Bella was living on a farm in the country. It wasn't easy to get to a therapist, so she used a self-regression tape:

I saw myself wearing that cloak in a lovely soft place of green hills and mists. I'm sure it was Ireland. I was the seer in a village. The people used to come to me with their questions and problems. I knew how to tune in and get answers for them from the gods and spirits of the land and they treated me with such high regard. That made me realize how much I've since got used to not getting any real respect from anyone.

I saw that the bloke I had dumped had been sent to wake me up. He didn't intend that with his ego self – it was organized from higher-self level. The blood in my eye was there to make sure I'd know that even though I'd confronted him on the astral plane, it had been a real event.

She told me what had happened since:

After that I started practising tuning in to get higher answers to various questions. I've now begun to read Tarot cards for people I know and they seem to like it. They've started sending their friends to me.

*And now that I'm here in Glastonbury, I've seen a cloak
in a shop that reminds me of the one in the dream. I
think I might just get it while I'm here.*

In the symbolic language of dreams, Bella's eye was affected
because she needed to see herself differently. Her inner
spirit wanted her to reclaim the dignity and higher powers
that she'd had in the past life in Ireland.

Astral experiences affect our material bodies in many
different ways. They can even create healing. Years ago, I
had a sty on one eye. I asked for a dream to heal it.

That night, I dreamed I met a friend while walking down
the road and he asked why I was wearing dark glasses. I said
it was to hide the sty. He told me to look at it in a mirror.

I took off the sunglasses and looked into a reflective
plate-glass shop front. I was astonished to see that the sty
had disappeared.

When I woke up the next day, I was amazed at how much
smaller the sty was. A day or so later, it had gone altogether.

Dion Fortune called this effect astral repercussion, saying,
'I myself have many times found curiously patterned bruises
on my body after an astral skirmish.'

She also needed a crisis to wake her up to her destiny.

The Making of a Magician

In 1911, at the age of 20, Dion Fortune, then still called
Violet Firth, went to teach in a private school. It was run by
a domineering woman who'd studied magic in India and
used hypnotic techniques to control her staff.

Although still naïve about what was really happening,
Dion Fortune knew something was wrong – a strange kind
of bullying was going on. After several arguments with the
head teacher, she decided to resign.

A co-worker advised her to just disappear, saying if she tried to leave openly she'd never get away. The young rebel didn't take that advice: she marched into the principal's office and announced that she was giving in her notice.

The older woman said that was fine, as long as she first admitted that she was incompetent and had no self-confidence. The junior hotly denied this. The head teacher then fixed her eyes with an intense stare. For nearly four hours she repeated the same accusations over and over again.

Afterwards Dion Fortune said this was more than just hypnosis, it was also telepathic thought transference. In other words, it was a massive, head-on psychic attack.

For the next three years the young teacher was debilitated and ill. She said she felt like an electric battery that had gone flat. She stayed on at the school, working like a drained and half-conscious automaton. It took her a long time to understand what had happened and start to recover.

During that time she began to study psychology and the occult. That was what finally turned her around. It not only restored her health but also gave her new strength and put her onto her destined path in life.

After a gruelling test, she'd drawn her sword from the stone and earned her magic cloak. It was the start of her transformation from Violet Firth into Dion Fortune – one of the most powerful and positive occultists of the last 100 years.

Many of us have been through similar experiences in past lives. Sometimes we only need a symbolic reminder to prod awake our old awareness.

The Curse

Jody came for a regression because of a strange phobia: whenever she saw a flock of birds in the distance, she felt so anxious she had to go inside to hide from them. If she wasn't near her home, she'd duck into the nearest shop.

At the time, she lived in the West Country and everyone she knew loved to watch the huge flocks of starlings that fly over that area in November. Disappointed that she couldn't share this pleasure, Jody wondered if her phobia was to do with a past-life experience. Her regression provided some surprising answers.

She recalled being a serving girl in a wealthy house in India, peeping through a grille from a cramped upper passage and nervously watching her employer in the room below:

He's kneeling in front of a little... altar, I think. He's got a lot of incense burning. I'm scared to move in case he hears me. He mutters some things, bows three times and then does it again. He's been doing that over and over.

Now he's taking something out of a bag and holding it up above his head. (Gasps) It's one of the kittens! He's chanting much faster now, still holding the kitten up in the air. Oh! He suddenly pushed the kitten onto the altar and cut its throat. He's collecting the blood in a dish – licking it off his fingers.

I must go quickly, quickly. He must never know what I've seen. Nobody must ever find out...

Oh no! Getting up too quickly, I made a little noise – and now he's looking straight up at this grille. I'm keeping very still, trying not to breathe. He's still looking up here. I don't know how much he can see. My heart is beating so loudly I'm sure he can hear it.

Alright, he's looked away now. He's clearing his things up. I must get away from here. He might come straight up here to see if anyone saw him. There's a little window at the end. I'm going to try and squeeze through it and get down from there.

AF: *What would he do if he caught you?*

J: *It would be bad enough just to find me not doing my work. For that alone I would be punished. But if he knows what I saw – aaay, my life would be over.*

I'm one of the youngest servants here. I come from a lowly background. My people are very poor. They gave me to this house as a servant when I was still young. They were crying, but they said it would give me a better life than I could ever have with them.

If I'm thrown out of here, no other house will take me and there's no other work I can do – I'd end up begging on the streets. So I'm very afraid of the master – especially after what I just saw.

With a few scratches, she managed to wriggle out of the tiny window and slip back to her work in the kitchen without anyone noticing. That evening she helped to clear the dishes from the family's evening meal – and was disturbed by the way the master was looking at her.

A few days later, he told her that he was a man of great knowledge and had powers she knew nothing about. She had sleepless nights worrying what that meant.

About a week later, she was alone in the orchard picking fruit for the cook when:

Oh no, here he comes again! I want to run away.

He stops to pick a fruit. He's eating it and staring at me.

He picks another fruit now. He comes to me and puts it into my bag. He leaves his hand in the bag and is playing with the fruit in there and laughing. I don't know what to do.

The next thing, her employer closed in and put his hand on her breast. No man had ever done that before. Panicking, she pushed him off and ran away.

She went to the little shrine in the servants' courtyard and prayed to Shiva for protection.

After that, nothing happened for a while. She thought that was because Shiva was answering her constant prayers. But then events moved forward:

There's an old Brahmin who's here quite a lot – a holy man. I think he comes to teach the children. He saw me praying at the little shrine and smiled at me. I think he was pleased with my devotion. That made me feel nice.

But then I had to go and clean the room where the master killed the kitten.

While I was doing that, the master came quietly into the room and crept up on me. I heard a little noise and when I looked round, he was standing right over me. I was so afraid. I thought, Now he will kill me like that kitten.

He told me to lie down at his feet, but I wouldn't. He kept saying he was a powerful man and no one could resist him. He tried to push me back onto the floor.

I was afraid for my life. I screamed and jumped up and pushed him away. He fell backwards over a big bowl onto the floor. As he lay on his back with his feet in the air, I ran away.

There is no doubt he will hate me now. I am finished. I went and lay flat in front of the servants' shrine and gave my life up to Shiva. I said, 'Whatever happens now, my life is in Shiva's hands.' I cried and cried. After a while I fell asleep, still lying there.

When I woke up it was dark. I knew that my life was over. But the spirit of Shiva had filled me. Nothing mattered anymore. I felt completely unafraid. I let Shiva direct my actions.

I went back into the main house. There was a big antique scimitar on the wall. I took it down. I felt its edge – it was still sharp. I took it and started to walk, as if in a dream, to where the master slept.

Then I heard a little cough behind me. I turned round. It was the Brahmin. He said, 'Sister, put that sword down.'

He'd never called me 'sister' before. Nobody here ever called me 'sister'. But I turned away from him and kept walking.

He came up behind me, grabbed my arms and made me drop the scimitar. I struggled and fought and tried to scratch him. He was talking all the time, but I wasn't listening.

In the end I couldn't fight him anymore. All the strength left me. I fell on the floor and started to weep. He was saying, 'Get up, get up, you must get your things and leave.' He was yanking me by the arm.

He pulled me back to my room and said I had to quickly pack my things.

So I was being thrown out onto the street! But I didn't care. My life had ended when I saw that kitten die. It might as well have been me.

I tied my things into a shawl. The Brahmin took me to the front door and pushed me outside. I thought he was going to lock me out, but he came with me and shut the door behind us. He said, 'We have a long way to go.'

After walking for a long time, he said we had to sit down and rest. I asked him if he was taking me to prison. He said, 'I am taking you away from a prison.' He told me he'd been watching and knew what was going on. He said that he saw I had a pure spirit, so he was taking me to where I really could serve Shiva.

We walked for the rest of the night. Along the way he talked about holy matters, but I was feeling so confused, it was hard for me to pay attention.

When dawn broke, she saw that they were heading for a country temple. The Brahmin took her into it and spoke to the priest for a long time. The temple was the most beautiful place she'd ever seen. The priest came and asked her if she'd like to stay there and help out with general duties. She was overwhelmed with gratitude.

He asked me a lot of questions and I told him everything that had happened. He said that man might still be dangerous for me and I had to stay inside the temple for a while and not go outside at all until he said I could.

She worked happily at the temple and stayed inside for several months as the priest had instructed. Then, one day:

I don't know what to do. There's no one here today to fetch the water from the well, but we need it for lots of things. If I go out quickly maybe it'll be alright. Maybe the priest just forgot to tell me that I can go outside now.

(Pause)

I'm walking down to the well with the buckets. It's nice to feel the hot sun on my arms again. The ground is warm under my feet. I can hear some insects making a loud singing noise. It's getting louder.

I look up. It's a big swarm. It makes a dark shape in the sky. There's something horrible about its shape. It's getting closer... bigger and louder. It's coming here – I think it's coming for me! I must run!

(Pause)

I turned to run and tripped and fell over. The swarm fell on me like a net and started stinging me.

I'm now lying on my mattress in my little room. People are here. I'm covered in stings. I can only see out of one eye. The priest says I should never have gone outside. The curse from that man was still waiting for me.

(A few weeks later)

The stings are gone now. The people here gave me things to make it better. The priest told me that my old master had sent a curse to me using the insects. He said he now knows that unless I face it and send it away, it'll never leave me alone. I'll never be safe.

He's started teaching me how to stand up to it. I have to learn to have strong faith in myself and Lord Shiva. Then I can use certain hand movements and words that will send the curse back where it came from. But if my faith isn't strong enough, nothing will work and the curse will destroy me. So he's giving me lots of stories and exercises and tests to strengthen my faith.

(A few weeks later)

The priest said, 'Today's lesson is outside.' He opened the door and I walked out. It was so nice to be in the open air again, feeling the sun on my skin and hearing the sounds of birds and monkeys in the trees.

Then I heard that buzzing sound again. It was far off, but it was getting louder. I remembered what I was supposed to do. I turned to face the evil noise with my hands held in a certain way and started chanting the secret things.

But the swarm still kept coming towards me. It got louder. I thought, This isn't going to work. I'm going to be attacked again. My heart felt so faint.

Then I suddenly felt angry. Why should I be attacked? I never did that man any harm. And I did something that the priest had never trained me to do: I shouted out all my anger in a great big 'HAH!' and used my hands to throw that at the swarm with all my might.

I heard a monkey scream in the trees and the swarm of insects turned away. They went over to the river on the other side and their sound faded.

The priest came out, smiling. He said, 'You've done it – you've sent it away. It won't come back again.'

(Pause)

I'm getting an overview of that life now. It's as though several years are going by quickly. I'm at the temple all the time, working there. I'm very happy... I do the cooking now, not the cleaning, so I'm not such a lowly person anymore.

People often come to the temple to speak to the priest about their problems. I let them in when they come to the door. Then I call the priest. He takes them to the visitors' room and I bring them tea and my little cakes.

I'm allowed to sit and watch from the corner. When they've gone, the priest talks to me about them. He's been teaching me how to see underneath what they say, what signs to look for – in their eyes, their words, their bodies – and other signs as well. I'm learning so much.

I now understand how that curse got put on me. I can see now when people are under a curse and don't know it. It happens when someone who knows them secretly wishes them evil. It goes on everywhere. Many people do black magic without knowing it.

I'm learning that everyone has what we call magical powers, even though they don't know it.

I am so happy to be learning these things. I thank Shiva every day for how my life has worked out.

Jody was delighted to have got to the bottom of her strange fear.

'It's not really about birds at all,' she said, 'it's because from a distance they look like a swarm of insects. That reminded me of that curse. Next year I'm going to make sure I go out and watch the starlings. I'm determined to get over this now.'

She was also fascinated by what she'd learned in the temple.

'I've always been interested in magic, but more from the psychological point of view. I'd love to train in something like that.'

We talked a bit about the possibilities and Jody finally decided to let her inner self lead her to whatever courses or books would help her on that path.

'I'm going to carry on where I left off in that life,' she said. 'Maybe that fear was a good thing in a way, because it's led me to what I really want to do in this life.'

Our personal wake-up calls grow directly from the soul journey, enriched by all our past-life experiences. They come when it's time to go through a special gate to a new and more magical part of the garden.

The inner self knows exactly where to find our personal gateways, whether they're in Edwardian schools, Indian temples or the Australian outback. Our lives send us to those places when we have enough inner resources to rise to the challenges that await us there.

Those challenges are the guardians of the gate. The only way past them is to realize that this is a spiritual test. It can't be solved in normal ways.

Once you see that, you know what to do. You draw the sword of spiritual awareness out of the stone of earthly consciousness. Then you can go through the gateway and into the magic garden. This is your true heritage – and the beginning of a higher phase of your soul journey.

PROTECTING YOURSELF FROM PSYCHIC ATTACK

The biggest sign of a psychic attack is when unusually negative thoughts start coming into your mind – especially if they happen to be about you. Other indications can be frequent nightmares, small accidents or feeling exhausted and under a dark cloud.

A psychic attack works best when you are unconscious of it. Becoming aware of it immediately weakens it and puts you in a position of strength.

You can then use some or all of the following to clear the last traces of it from your life:

- First thing in the morning and last thing at night, say, 'I call on higher light to protect me at all times.' See a pyramid of blue light surrounding you. This shield will stay in place and deflect any attacks aimed at you.

- Make a list of everything about yourself and your life that is good, happy and positive. Read it often and keep adding to it.

- Imagine the attack as a pathetic, ugly little creature. Say, 'I wish you peace. Be on your way,' and send it a sphere of light. See the light surrounding it and floating it far away. Watch it getting smaller and smaller until it disappears altogether.

- See a bright light expanding from your heart centre until it completely fills and surrounds you. Say, 'My aura is strong and clear.'

- Focus on cheerful and life-affirming books, films and information.

- Find things to laugh about – laughter is a powerful dispeller of negativity.

- See the experience as a blessing in disguise. The deeper reason it came into your life was to prompt you to own your inner powers and reclaim your true potential.

23

HIDDEN TESTS

After the fledgling magician has faced down the guardians of the gate, they enter the magic garden and a new life opens up. An exciting world of wonder lies ahead to be explored. Yet subtle tests and hidden pitfalls line the pathways.

This is what the Tarot card of the Fool depicts. It shows a young person happily setting off on a journey. Holding a flower aloft, his face is turned idealistically towards the skies. It's a sunny day, but sharp, icy crags loom in the background. The Fool, not looking where he's going, is about to step over a cliff. A little dog is trying to warn him, but it looks as though he's about to tumble into the first pitfall on the path.

What are these hidden hazards? In a nutshell, they are the temptations of using magical knowledge and powers to serve the lower self.

In *The Elixir and the Stone*, authors Michael Baigent and Richard Leigh analyse the difference between sacred and profane magicians. For them, a profane magician is one who thinks of supernatural forces as a resource to use and control, acting in a detached way, like a scientist doing vivisection.

Most medieval magicians worked in that way. They began their rituals by solemnly drawing a protective line around themselves. They'd then call up spirits of doubtful origin and issue them with commands. Unaware of themselves in any deeper ways, they assumed that the forces they unleashed had little to do with them and couldn't affect them.

During the Renaissance, the emphasis shifted from trying to dominate otherworldly forces to understanding them. Magicians were beginning to realize that affecting the world out there began from within.

The sixteenth-century physician and alchemist Paracelsus was a good example of this new kind of sacred magician. He understood how the imagination affected the body and was a pioneer of holistic medicine. He said he helped to cure his patients by healing the aspect within himself that the patient mirrored.

With Paracelsus and others like him, the old shamanic ideal of the wounded healer was starting to come back.

Many people hesitate to use their own powers, saying they're convinced they misused them in a previous life, so must never use them again. However, I've come to doubt that's true for everyone who feels that way. Those feelings may be the signs of other, more subtle tests.

Sometimes people fear their inner powers because of past and present-life cultural conditioning. Although it varies around the world, in most places power of any kind has always been more taboo for females. Both men and women may carry old wounds because of that and feel that magic is forbidden to them.

Deeply religious past lives may also come up to test us at key moments. Just when we're about to delve into esoteric mysteries, our past-life priests, monks or nuns suddenly wake up! Whether they're our old selves or people we once respected, with the power of the subconscious they can send us disturbing messages about the evil nature of our new interests.

In some cases, this worry may be more about the future than the past. The real fear might be: once we've claimed our inner powers, how will we use them?

The Rival

Ilana, who lived on a beautiful tropical island, was miserable about her husband's open long-term affair with another woman. In her regression, she sensed ancient mysterious knowledge lying deep within her psyche. She also glimpsed times when she knew how to use that power. At that point, she shut it all down. She said she didn't want to know any more about it and asked me to bring her out of the regression.

Afterwards Ilana said she'd always felt that magic wasn't allowed for her now because she once used it wrongly. As we talked, a bigger fear slowly came out: what she might do to her love rival if she did get her old power back. Her island home was a place where people constantly used petty black magic against each other, so she knew its power and potential.

In the end, we decided that she first needed to resolve her relationship issues. Once she'd done that, she might feel ready to explore her ancient knowledge again.

The Too-High Priest

Sometimes people are afraid of their inner power because deep down they know that the time has come to reclaim it. Life is pushing them steadily in that direction, but to move ahead they must break through the mysterious barrier that's holding them back.

Elderly Joanna told me that despite having a comfortable life with good friends, she'd been depressed for a long time. The main problem seemed to be her husband. She described how he'd occasionally take on the persona of an Old Testament-style prophet. During those times she said he uttered 'great truths', but behaved in even less considerate ways than usual. From what she told me, his everyday self sounded intelligent, manipulative and waspish. He was especially good at making her feel in the wrong all the time.

In the regression she went back to a life as a young girl in ancient Egypt. She'd almost worshipped her present husband, who had been a great high priest at the time. In that life, becoming his wife one day would have seemed beyond her wildest dreams.

Joanna's spirit guide showed her that in subsequent incarnations she and the high priest had gone their separate ways. She'd followed her higher path and evolved to become her own wise inner priestess. In contrast, he'd spiralled downward with an increasingly inflated ego about his spiritual role.

This life was her big test. Faced with her high priest again, she'd shrunk back into the timid devotee of old. Unless she resolved this, the progress she'd made for so many lifetimes would be lost.

Her guide said Joanna had the power to move both herself and her husband out of the shadow selves that they now occupied. She could do that by refusing to be a bullied little wife and placing more trust in her own intuition and inner wisdom.

Afterwards Joanna said knowing the history of the relationship had helped her a lot. Although it might take a while, she was sure she'd manage this change now that she knew how important it was.

Many people feel squashed for the same reason: somewhere along the line, an overbearing guru has made them feel inferior. So they slide into the trap of disempowerment. But once they've realized that, the way ahead becomes clear.

The Psychic Soldier

The esoteric path is littered with common tests and hurdles, but the way we put them together will be uniquely our own.

Lynne, a soldier, told me that she was haunted by past-life dabblings in black magic – and persistent feelings of still being drawn to it. Despite a lifetime of resisting these feelings, she worried that she might have accidentally cursed others with her anger.

On the positive side, she said she could walk into a room full of strangers and sense which of them would be friendly to her. She could also see through the masks of certain popular people to the dark underside that no one else saw.

Her regression was difficult because she was blocked with tension about what might come up.

She first saw herself walking along a muddy path in complete darkness. Someone or something powerful was following her, but when she turned around she didn't see anything. She said this happened in her ordinary life as well.

I wondered if her issue about black magic was haunting her because it needed to be resolved. I suggested that she look at a key past-life event as a detached observer – like watching a film.

When she did this, Lynne saw a man strangling a woman. He was screaming at her for being an evil witch.

Lynne knew she was that woman. It reminded her of how furious she'd been at the time – and still was. With the anger came a physical feeling of something heavy closing up her throat.

The way we die can leave a deep impression on the psyche that lasts until we work with the memory. Death by strangling affects the throat chakra, making self-expression difficult in later lives. Lynne and I worked on healing those wounds and did visualizations to dissolve the anger that she'd been holding deep inside herself for so long.

As we chatted afterwards, it became clear why she'd taken up soldiering. Army life would surely keep her well away from the occult and might even redeem her in some way. There was an element of self-sacrifice to it. She said she knew the work would kill her and she was happy about that. It seemed that although she was still unconsciously fuming about her past-life death, it had imprinted her with the idea that she was an evil witch and deserved to die.

I suggested that a better solution might be to see the good side of her innate potential – and to decide that whatever might or might not have happened in the past, she would now use her powers in positive ways.

Leaving this life is no solution to a problem – the same issue will only come up again next time around. It's easier to sort it out now.

Lynne saw the sense of that and left in a thoughtful mood.

The Angel and the Devil

Most people's fears about the dark side of their latent powers are usually just that – fears. But what if you really did make a past-life pact with the devil? What happens then? Olivia's regression gave some surprising answers to those questions.

She recalled being a waif-like girl of about 13. She'd been locked into a shed for some misdemeanour. Her clothes were thin and it was cold. She was frightened and hungry.

Then she had 'an infusion of energy' that changed her mood and made her more determined. After that, she managed to escape – but couldn't recall exactly how. A curtain had come down over that part of her memory and nothing could budge it.

The next significant thing she recalled was when she'd grown into a beautiful young woman. She was wearing a rich red dress and an artist was painting her portrait. From the look of the clothes, this was sometime in the seventeenth century.

The red dress was important to her. I think that's how she saw herself. And how she wanted to be seen.

(Slowly and hesitantly) This woman is quite authoritative. She's used to giving commands. She's not at all how we think women were in those days.

And there's – there's another side to her, quite a dark side. She can use her will-power in some way to get what she wants.

But it's also more than that – it's something from the outside. She might have been possessed – inhabited by a demonic being which sometimes came to the fore.

AF: *How did that work?*

O: *She conjured up this force initially from inside her. It then came to her. It's a very strong power and she applied it with great force of will. It got her anything she wanted – anything at all.*

AF: *How did she do that?*

O: *She raised one fist in the air and her face completely changed. The person she was using this energy on would be terrified of her.*

When she drew on this power – when the other being took control – her eyes changed. They went very wide and the whites changed to green.

Later the person upon whom she had used the power would blank the incident out. They'd forget all about it, because it seemed impossible. They'd believe that they'd given her the horse, or whatever she'd wanted, because she was pretty and charming. Their rational mind wouldn't accept that she'd terrified them with her dominating power of evil.

AF: What kind of things did she get with this power?

O: She used it to get a beautiful chestnut horse. She rode it side-saddle. She could get any man she wanted. Everything she had, she got from this power and from the force of her will.

She lived in luxurious surroundings, with exquisite fabrics, beautiful furniture and pleasant people around her. I can see her with wealthy-looking people, drinking tea out of tiny cups.

AF: Did she belong to some kind of esoteric or secret group?

O: No. But she may have been taught these things by... maybe what she would call a demonic being.

(The memory then moved to the following incident.)

I'm suddenly aware of a giant angel – very tall, and pointing upwards, completely detached and non-emotional – almost stony-faced.

The woman is crouching on the floor near its feet, looking downwards. She appears cowed, but in fact she's gathering her power. She's aware that she'll have to draw on a really enormous amount of power to stand up to this gigantic angel.

The part of the house immediately around the woman is in the bright colours and rich fabrics of her choice. But around the angel, the house is ruined and bleak. It's open to the sky and colourless. There are just rotting timber beams that look like ribs.

It's as if the angel has come to replace her illusory reality with the true situation. She's going to need a huge amount of power to stop that happening.

She stands up slowly. The angel is pointing up. As if in obedience, she starts to go up the stairs. But she has a plan. When she reaches the first landing she stands there, facing the angel.

She is now in a higher position. She uses her power to draw all the colours and richness of her chosen reality with her. This starts to cancel out the effects of the angel.

Then she goes up the second flight of stairs, stops again at the top and does that again – draws her whole world of richness and colour up with her. This has the effect of painting out the kind of world the angel is bringing.

She continues to use her power to spread the colour and luxury and richness to an increasing area. The colour expands and expands until it reaches the very top of the house. It then obliterates the angel completely. It is as if it has been painted over.

(Long silence.)

It's now the end of her life. She's in a bed at the top of the house. The scene around her is partly the usual luxury and richness, but in patches there are bare timbers. There's a fading in and out, as if she can no longer focus her will all the time on maintaining her world.

She's expecting the devil to come at her death to collect her.

AF: *How does she feel about that?*

O: *She feels that he is her master and her friend.*

(Pause)

At my death, the roof of the room split open. A huge figure of a devil appeared – much taller than the house.

He reached out for me. Although I welcomed this at first, it soon became clear that instead of welcoming me home as a friend and loyal servant, he was maliciously laughing at me – at my naïve belief that I would be treated well by him.

I screamed in fear and horror. He laughed mockingly and scooped me up in a large hand that was as big as my whole body.

(Long pause)

I'm now floating in a kind of liquid that's helping me in some way. It's black with long glittering streaks of bright blue and other colours. I'm only semi-conscious. The effect is soothing.

(That apparently continued for some time. We moved to the next development.)

I'm aware of an arched doorway with pale pinky-goldy light shining through it. I go through that doorway and into another room. There's a beautiful statue of an angel here. It's holding up a lantern and writing in an open book.

This room is very large and full of arches. I get the word 'classroom', although it doesn't look like one. The lighting is subdued and diffuse. There are sofas here and there, and a few people. Two people are talking together on one of the sofas. It feels as if one of them is helping the other in some way.

I move slowly through this big area. Then I see another light source from an arched doorway. I go through there, down some stairs and into the back of a lecture theatre.

There are rows of fixed chairs facing away from me, sloping down towards the stage at the bottom. Quite a few people are sitting here. Some of them are on their own, others are in *pairs or small groups. Some have pencils and paper, as if to take notes.*

I take a seat near the back. My foot is tapping nervously. Someone comes to the lectern to give a talk. He looks like an old-fashioned doctor – someone people would be inclined to trust, anyway. I'm not sure what he's saying. I get the impression it's reassuring stuff.

AF: *Is this a memory of another life or are you still in the after-life place?*

O: *This is still the after-life place. I'm still that woman, more or less. This isn't a new physical life.*

AF: *Did the talk explain where you are?*

O: *Not directly, no. They let you know things more subtly than that. The feeling I get is that everyone is left to realize what they need to, in their own time, as they go along. Some of them are aware that this is the situation and they've adjusted to it, like the ones who've come with notepaper and pencils, but there are others who are looking rather bewildered and disorientated. They're staring around a bit, as if not sure where they are or why. They're not overly alarmed, though, because so far it seems unthreatening and even safe in a vaguely familiar way. The whole set-up seems designed to reassure – to give a semblance of normality.*

After the talk we all get up and file down the steps of the central aisle towards the stage. At the bottom we leave the lecture theatre by a side door and go through a room. It has several pairs of large doors in the walls. They look like the doors to huge ovens or kilns. But we just pass through that room.

Olivia said it was then like being shown round a huge stately home. Every room represented a different period in history.

During this tour, she began to relax a bit more. After that, her memory moved to the next phase:

> *I'm now in a pink room. We're all lying on comfortable sofas under silky coverlets. Everything's in warm shades of pink. The colour is significant. It's part of a healing process.*
>
> *There are slightly old-fashioned looking nurses tending to us all. I think that's just how I see them. In reality, they are benign entities, like angels. They are healing and repairing us.*
>
> **AF:** *How are you feeling now?*
>
> **O:** *Exhausted – completely exhausted. But it feels alright now. I'm at peace at last.*

Olivia later returned for another regression. We didn't see any more of the woman in the red dress. Instead, she was granted an overview of her soul journey – and what looked like a symbolic preview of the future:

> *I'm walking through a forest. There is wind, darkness and great danger here. I'm following a little path. I have a small light in a glass globe. I'm carrying it with both hands, as though it is something precious.*
>
> *This light was forged aeons ago. I've carried it through countless lifetimes. It was part of my knowledge of the Earth when I was a primitive hunter. It was hidden in my orthodox bag when I was a darkly clerical man. It was among my baubles when I was a bright young thing in the 1920s. It has always been with me.*
>
> *As I walk through the woods, I can feel elf hands plucking at my coat sleeves. It's so important that I not be distracted from my path – my purpose – that I let them have the coat, and keep going. It's better to lose the coat than let anything lead me from my path.*

I'm taking this light to a fire. When I get there, I'll put it onto that fire. Then the light will become so bright and so brilliant I'll finally be able to read a book that was always closed to me before.

(Pause)

Now I can see a long row of people in different historical dress. I'm driving along a road with those people on either side. They're all cheering. There's a great feeling of victory and success. It feels as though the higher spiritual purpose of those lives has won through, despite all the dangers.

This hasn't happened yet, but it will.

Olivia felt that this had been shown to her to reassure her about the earlier memory she'd got. That had been preying on her mind a bit, despite knowing that after that life she'd been healed and repaired, not judged or punished.

The message that her inner light had always been with her and her soul mission would be successful gave her a lovely sense of peace about all her lives. It was a wonderful feeling that somehow, in the end, all would be well.

This happy ending applies to everyone. Whatever pitfalls we stumble into, all is forgiven in the end. Earth is like a school. Mistakes are part of the learning process.

People's memories of the between-life worlds have made it clear that we are the only ones who punish ourselves for our shortcomings. The realms of angels and spirit guides respond to our errors with love and healing.

However long it takes, one day we'll all graduate from this amazing school. Then we'll be able to look back, swap notes and reminisce about all the adventures we had while we were here. I'm sure we'll agree it was worth it. Earth is a top-quality school – this is why we chose to come here in the first place.

24

THE RETURN OF THE MAGICIAN

Pulling the sword from the stone represents an initiatory experience – the beginning of a new path. The mighty sword of Excalibur comes later. It stands for fully developed magical power.

In the legend, the Lady of the Lake offers Excalibur to Arthur. He has to row out onto the lake to receive it from her. She represents the moon side of consciousness: intuition and the knowing of the heart. The lake symbolizes the unconscious depths of the psyche – the true source of Excalibur's power.

At first, Arthur's knights are true to their noble mission. But after a while, personal frailties creep in and slowly take over. In the end, the dark side of human nature destroys the Round Table.

The final blow comes when Arthur is grievously wounded. He stands for our rightful heritage – the magical power that comes from accessing the full 'round table' of our greater consciousness. If that falls apart, the king also falls. Awareness of our higher potential dims and is forgotten. To stop its powers being abused, Excalibur must return to the lake.

In the legend, the weakened Arthur asked Sir Bedivere to perform this sacred task. Bedivere was the knight who was most drawn to black magic. Dazzled by the splendour and power of Excalibur, he secretly decided not to throw it away and hid it instead. But Arthur knew and sent him back. The third time, Bedivere finally flung Excalibur into the lake.

At that point, a hand – 'clothed in white samite, mystic, wonderful', as Tennyson described it – reached up, took the sword and drew it down into the deeps. This was a sign that Excalibur would not be lost. The Lady of the Lake would keep it safe until the time came to offer it again.

Three hooded women in black then arrived on a barge. They took Arthur over the water to the Isle of Avalon. There he would heal and prepare to return one day to be the rightful king again.

Written versions of this story began to come out from the ninth century onwards. The original legend, however, comes from the oral tradition of a much older mythology.

Myths and legends are like maps for the spiritual journey. They give meaning to the personal path. The concept of the good and rightful king waiting to return expresses some of our deepest instincts about ourselves.

In our inmost hearts we know that a time will come when our true, good nature will be 'king' – the rightful ruler of our round table of personal traits. When that happens, Excalibur will return.

After Arthur had gone, Bedivere retired to a hermitage for the rest of his life. Guinevere went into a convent. This reflects the times when we distrust our magic powers and take lives sheltering within the safety of religion. Eventually life will push us into trying our wings again. But it pushes gently and prepares us slowly.

The Golden Key

Sometimes the first step is a symbolic one. In Jenna's regression, she was standing on a dark Victorian city street, feeling like an outcast and looking wistfully into the window of a house.

Inside, she saw a man who looked different from anyone else. He had a long white beard and wore a hooded robe, like a wizard. He knew she could see him, although nobody else could.

He smiled at her and spun a globe of the world. Jenna felt this meant time had passed, the world had moved on and she was now welcome. She was then standing in that room with him.

He gave her a golden key. It was the key to her greater Self.

She wrapped up an old past-life memory and put it into a box. Then she used the key to open a cupboard. She put the memory into the cupboard, to join many other memories that had been wrapped up and put away there.

That memory had been holding her back for a long time. Now it would no longer bother her. She was allowed to finally put it away. She said she felt so much lighter after that – it was a great relief.

Although she didn't see what that memory was about, she knew it had been a block on her path, preventing her from reclaiming her ancient knowledge and abilities. The positive symbol of a smiling magician giving her a golden key had replaced it.

Jenna said this reassured her that she was on a path that was being watched over in a good way. She felt that when she was ready to take the next step, her kindly wizard would guide her through it.

The Exorcist

When the right moment comes, life can steer our paths in unexpectedly dramatic ways. One afternoon in late autumn I was walking up Glastonbury High Street when I bumped into an old friend. He said it was perfect synchronicity, as he had something extraordinary to tell me.

We went to a nearby candlelit café so we could talk over mugs of hot chocolate. He told me that in his meditations he'd been getting information about a certain place in the West Country that was still a focus of evil power. It was somehow connected with the Knights Templar. He thought they might have been betrayed and killed there.

He was worried about this message and had been wondering whether to dismiss it or do something about it. Doing something meant calling on magical power to remove the evil in the place, so that negative forces could no longer use it. But he'd rejected the ways of magic long ago. They didn't belong to his higher path. So he was in a dilemma.

He said he'd asked and asked for a sign that would show him the best way ahead. Then, on a train journey to London, he'd watched the following scene unfold:

> A man in a business suit was sitting diagonally opposite a woman. She was also conventionally dressed. They weren't together. After a few moments they had some sort of brief exchange, but I didn't hear what it was.
>
> The man then retired behind his newspaper. The woman became very angry. She started flicking her fingers aggressively at his paper. He ignored it. She rolled up her own newspaper and started slapping it loudly on her palm. He ignored that as well. Then she made strong movements with her hands, very obviously beaming bad vibes at him. The man ignored her the whole time.

The next time the train stopped, she got off. All the others in the carriage gave the man a round of applause.

I said maybe he should go and see an exorcist now. He calmly replied, 'I am an exorcist.'

I'm sure this was the sign I'd been asking for. But I'd appreciate discussing it a bit. I want to make sure that I'm not jumping to the wrong conclusions.

We talked the whole matter through for some time and in the end we decided that this was his call to action. Life was asking him to reclaim his ancient abilities to clear a patch of evil from the world. He knew he'd once had a past life as an exorcist and the incident on the train gave him a pointed reminder to own that again. He also had an old connection to the Templars, so this task was perfect for him.

Once he'd reconciled himself to the higher purpose of calling on magical power, he felt clear about it. Although he didn't talk about it much after that, he let me know that he was successful in the end.

Dark Forces

Just as a psychic attack can push us into drawing our sword from the stone, the iniquities of the world may be the only thing that finally gets us to reclaim our forgotten powers.

Keran called on me because of an odd but revealing incident. He'd been working quietly at his computer late one night when suddenly there was loud knocking on the curtained window next to him. He panicked and looked for somewhere to hide. When he found it had only been a neighbour, he realized he had to do something about this strange fear.

Throughout his life he'd had disturbing dreams about trying to escape an invisible pursuer. After this incident, the nightmares got worse. So he came for a regression to get to the bottom of it.

He recalled being a German man in early middle age around the time of the Second World War. He was on a train, trying to escape from Nazi Germany. It was extremely risky. It also meant leaving everything behind – his secure scientific job, as well as his home and family.

This drama had its roots in much earlier lives:

> *In some of my past lives I knew a lot about the occult.*
> *But at a certain point I decided against it, because I saw*
> *where that knowledge could lead. I saw what it could do.*
> *I came into this German life determined to shut it out. I took*
> *up science. I was going to stick to the rational intellect and*
> *material matters.*
>
> *And then, because of what's been going on in this country,*
> *the path of science led me back into the shadows. The occult*
> *is the new fashion round here, but in a secret way – not for*
> *the masses, only for the élite. I saw some bad stuff going on*
> *because of this. Then I was asked to do certain things that*
> *were against my conscience. I decided to get out.*
>
> *So here I am, sitting on this train. I wish it would get going*
> *again. I don't know why it's stopping here. We're not at a*
> *station. I can tell that we've stopped for a bad reason – a*
> *lifetime of trying to shut off this sixth sense hasn't worked.*
>
> *I can hear heavy footsteps in the corridor and the banging and*
> *rattling of compartment doors. The train is being searched.*
> *They're looking for someone. Maybe me. I'm hardly breathing.*
>
> **AF:** *Is anyone else in the compartment with you?*
>
> **K:** *Just an old peasant woman in the corner. She's busy eating*
> *from a basket of apples and looking out of the window.*

They're next door now. I can hear every word. The door slams. Now they're here. The door opens. Two soldiers. One of them demands my papers.

I'm reaching for the false papers that I've prepared... and... it's as if everything has switched to slow motion. It's very strange. I'm aware of every tiny detail. I can almost see what this soldier is thinking. Every little twitch in his face is perfectly clear. It's easy to see all the things that are normally so fast we aren't consciously aware of them.

I feel strangely confident – as if I know exactly what to do. I smile pleasantly at the soldier and give him the papers in a slightly muddled way. It's to confuse him for a moment. In that moment, without saying anything, I kind of radiate to him that I'm a very important German scientist who's doing crucial work to help us win the war.

He looks at my papers, but very briefly. I can tell he feels embarrassed to have to do this to someone like me. I respond by exuding a tolerant understanding towards him. He must do his war work, just as I am doing mine. I'm not offended. We are comrades in arms.

He gives my papers back, a bit apologetically. I nod to him like an approving superior. He salutes me with great formality and goes on his way.

The old woman is staring at me with a slightly open mouth. He didn't bother with her. They must be looking for a man. I still think it might be me.

I'm sinking back into normal consciousness now. It's as if I suddenly became filled up with extra power. And that power knew just what to do.

AF: *Have you ever done anything like that before?*

K: *No. Never. It just happened. It was a complete surprise, and very disturbing. I'm dabbing my face with a handkerchief.*

The old woman is looking at me a bit more shrewdly now. I must deflect this. I ask if she's selling those apples. She says yes. I give her a generous amount of money for three small apples. She's satisfied. She goes back to munching and looking out of the window.

I can hear the train guard blowing his whistle. I think we're moving now. Yes... slowly creaking into action again... picking up speed. The faster we go, the better I feel.

He managed to complete the tense and dangerous journey to England. There he gave himself up, was interrogated and told all he knew. After that he was interned for the rest of the war. He said it was rather dull, but the internees were treated reasonably.

After the war, he got a job in London. His wife had divorced him for being a traitor to the Fatherland, so he was alone in the world.

Then one misty afternoon he saw a little notice in a shop window advertising a talk by a psychic group.

I feel drawn to it. That worries me. I'm afraid of being pulled back into the occult. But a little talk should be harmless enough. I'm a bit isolated these days. Talks and societies are a good way to be with people.

And so he began going to that group's meetings. He felt they were a bit naïve, but it was cosy and companionable. After a while, the members of the group started encouraging him to share the esoteric knowledge they sensed he had but was keeping to himself. They'd ask for his advice and suggested that he give talks to the group now and then.

He found it hard to refuse because they'd treated him kindly. Without their acceptance, he would have been quite lonely. So he shared what he could with them – up to a point. He still feared being drawn back into the dark side of magic. Then one day a crisis came up:

Two of the ladies from the group have come to visit me. They're worried. They say they've both had warning dreams about one of the men in our group. I don't tell them this, but I've also felt uneasy about him. He's been trying to take over leadership of the group. I think he also wants to stand for parliament.

I've suspected for some time that he's been secretly using black magic to get his own way. And I think – I've seen some of the signs – that he's also being driven toward positions of power by some sort of dark force. But I've been keeping quiet about it.

Now these women are telling me some disturbing things about this man. He can't be trusted. They're asking me to use my knowledge to stop him. But that's like using black magic to stop black magic. I won't do that. I tell them I'll give it some careful thought.

I have to think very hard now. I somehow know that the choice I make about this will define the rest of my life, for better or worse. And I don't know what the best choice is.

(A few days later)

I'm entering a meeting of the group.

AF: *Have you made a decision about what the women asked you?*

K: *Yes.*

AF: *Have you told them?*

K: No. They look round at me as I walk in. I can see they're wondering what I'm going to do. I don't sit down as I would normally, but walk straight to the top of the room. The people who run these meetings are there, talking together in a little knot.

AF: Does that include the man the two women are worried about?

K: Yes. I break in on their talk. I say I have an important announcement to make. They look surprised, but then say OK – except for the man in question. I can see he's looking for a way to stop me. I must move quickly. So I go to the table and ask everyone to sit down.

Now he's found a way. He says, 'Hold on, hold on, you can't just take over like this. We have to discuss it and take a vote.'

The two women who came to me can see what's going on. They shout him down, saying that's not necessary. Others agree with them.

So I grab the moment and launch straight into it. I tell them that I've made a big decision. As soon as I say that, the room falls quiet. All eyes are on me.

I go on to explain that in distant past lives I may have used magic in a dark way – but I've now realized that to refuse to ever use my abilities again is not the answer. All that does is open the door for those who do use black magic. It gives them a clear run. They get no opposition from those who know what they're really up to. So I've decided to get back on the horse that threw me – and ride it properly this time.

As I say these things I'm starting to feel clearer than I've felt for a very long time. When I've finished, I end with a special dedication. I ask that this group and everyone in it will be aligned with the forces of light and that we'll seek not personal power but to be an instrument for good in the world.

It's a simple invocation, but because I've held back for so long it has a lot of energy. It seems to affect the people there quite strongly. When I've finished, they all stand up and clap and cheer.

AF: *Even the man in question?*

K: *Well, he has to stand up when everyone else does. And when he does, to some extent he automatically aligns himself with the dedication.*

The two women who spoke to me are looking happy. They come to me afterwards to thank me. I tell them we'll still have to wait and see what happens with this man. But they say they're not thanking me for that. They're thanking me for allowing myself to use magic again.

I feel as though a dark cloud that's been hanging over me all my life has finally gone.

Afterwards Keran shared his thoughts about this memory:

I can understand now why I was afraid of the banging on the window. At one level, it was my subconscious past-life fear of the Nazis coming after me. On another level, it was my own spirit trying to wake me up because it had something to tell me. I needed to become conscious of this memory – firstly to stop the nightmares about being pursued, and then to remember why it's a good thing to accept my old, esoteric knowledge again.

The Nazi party was basically a black magic organization. It was the militant wing of the occult Thule Society, which was spawned by the racist mysticism of the Ariosophy movement.

For those who could read them, the outer signs of Nazi occultism were obvious. The swastika is an ancient symbol of the life force. The Nazi salute was based on a magical ritual gesture of power. The great rallies were deliberate ceremonies of mass hypnotism.

Nobody knew what dark sorcery the Nazis got up to behind the scenes – but we can make some informed guesses. Using slave labour, Heinrich Himmler expanded the Castle of Wewelsburg to make it a formidable citadel that would be the centre of Nazi occult operations. Facing defeat in April 1945, he ordered the castle and its contents destroyed. He could not, however, demolish all the rumours about satanic rituals and human sacrifices that had taken place within its grim walls.

Dion Fortune said she only fully understood the true nature of the war after she'd read an unexpurgated version of Hitler's book *Mein Kampf*.

'Manipulation of the racial subconscious mind is one of the strongest cards they play,' she stated in *The Magical Battle of Britain*. 'This card can only be trumped by a higher card of the same denomination. Military force is ineffectual against it, and it is here that our specialised knowledge can be of very real use.'

She guided the Society of the Inner Light in London and Glastonbury to do this work throughout the war. She said it was vital not to hate the enemy: that only weakened the inner spirit and bound you to the hated one. And however evil they might seem to be, no one had the right to attack another.

'All we can do,' she said, 'is open a channel whereby spiritual forces are brought to bear upon the problem.'

Her followers did that by regularly sending light to the Nazis and visualizing Germany becoming a place of peace and goodwill. In addition, they called up huge angelic presences to guard and watch over Great Britain.

Other magic societies also shored up this esoteric protection. One of the strongest and best known was Dorothy

Clutterbuck's coven in the New Forest. Gerald Gardner, author of the influential *Witchcraft Today*, belonged to this circle. It played a central role at Lammas in August 1940, rallying groups throughout the country to ramp up the psychic defence during the critical Battle of Britain. Perhaps it was partly because of this invisible help that the relatively small RAF finally triumphed in that battle.

As a Druid, the wartime prime minister, Winston Churchill, had his own personal connections with the English esoteric milieu. Some say he was aware of their psychic war work and quietly supported it. During the darkest days of the war, he took the advice of the mystic Tudor Wellesley Pole of Glastonbury and instituted the 'silent minute'. At 9 p.m. every night, on the striking of Big Ben, the nation stopped all activities and focused its collective mind on peace. This was a powerful magical ritual, and Churchill probably knew it.

Many of the baby boom generation are the reincarnations of people who died in the war. It's no surprise that they grew up to drive the peace and love movement that has made such an impact on the world, or that they transformed Churchill's V-for-victory sign into the universal symbol of peace.

The Reunion

A few years ago I had this e-mail from an old friend I hadn't heard from in a long time:

> The other evening I had the most amazing vision. I must share it with you.
>
> I saw a figure in a deep blue hooded cloak. He was moving slowly along a little pathway next to a stone wall. I felt nervous about this for some reason, but I decided to face whatever it might be, so I carried on watching.

He went through a small gateway in the wall and into a large garden. It was neglected and overgrown. There was a big house there, also disused and broken down. It seemed to be a place he'd known when it was thriving. It might have been the home of some kind of community.

He moved slowly, taking in the whole scene. It felt as though he hadn't been back here for a long time.

He went round to the back and headed for a group of old oak trees. At the base of one of them was a hole, like a fairy doorway. He reached in there and pulled out a beautiful silver box. It was covered with mysterious etchings.

Slowly, he opened the box. In it there was a gold key. He held it up to the light with great joy. That was a big moment for him – it meant a lot to find it again.

He went further into the wild area of the back garden. After pushing away a lot of creepers, he found an old wooden door in the side of a hill. He unlocked it with the key and went in.

Inside there was a long passage. Small candles provided a flickering light. Old rugs were on the floor. At the end of this passage was a beautiful library, with ancient books lining the walls.

Standing there, as if waiting, was the woman in charge of this place. She was wearing a silver cloak and had a crescent moon on her forehead. They greeted each other warmly and embraced.

It was an emotional, joyful reunion. He was home at last, after many years of wandering in the wilderness.

Between them they'll now be able to restore the old house and garden and use them again. Their intention is to make them even better than they used to be.

I received the message that this is a vision of what's happening for everybody. It symbolizes a process that's slowly taking place at deep levels within the mass psyche. It means the old magic ways that were banned can now come back.

It'll be alright now. We don't need to be afraid of magic. It won't have to hide underground or be unconscious anymore. We can welcome the magician home again.

After countless past lives exploring the potential of magic, we're starting to understand what it really is. It always came from the power of the mind – the lake of Arthurian legend. Spells worked primarily because people intended them to, and believed that they would. Intent has great power.

'Once you make a decision, the universe conspires to make it happen,' said Ralph Waldo Emerson.

What we call 'magic' is this natural ability of consciousness to affect reality. It goes on unconsciously all the time. Our thoughts, decisions, attitudes and beliefs have more power than most of us realize.

'Magic is believing in yourself,' said Goethe. 'If you can do that, you can make anything happen.'

It's said that psychic abilities are a curse when you don't own them and a blessing when you do. I'd say that applies to all the powers of the mind – especially the imagination.

Many people are now beginning to realize that we can inadvertently harm ourselves and others by dwelling on fears and negative imagery. We're learning how important it is to be joyful, positive and loving in order to attract similar vibrations into our lives.

The culmination of all our past-life experiences of magic is to realize that these abilities are our natural heritage and birthright. We use them all the time – even when we aren't aware of it.

We are all magicians, and always were. When we own that power, we can start using it consciously to make a better world for all.

YOUR PAST-LIFE MAGICIAN MEMORIES

Once more, this visualization will introduce you to your past-life memories in a safe and gentle way. You'll be able to view scenes from your past lives as a detached observer, without needing to relive any of the experiences. Whenever you wish, you can stop the exercise simply by opening your eyes. For extra reassurance, ask your guardian angel or spirit guide to be with you.

Repeat this exercise whenever it feels right. At first you may get only brief glimpses of your memories, but with practice you'll gather a lot of information about your past lives. As you go along, you'll begin to see the bigger picture of your soul's reincarnational journey. This will help you to understand much more about your current life and how it fits into your higher purpose.

- ◉ *Preparation:* Sit or lie somewhere where you can be quiet and undisturbed.

- ◉ *Relaxation:* Scrunch up and expand all your muscles – especially your face, hands, arms and shoulders. Then let all your muscles soften and relax.

- ◉ *Focus:* Become aware of everything that's underneath you. Sense how comfortable, firm and supportive it is.

- ◉ *Centre yourself:* Gaze steadily at a candle or a crystal until you want to close your eyes.

- ◉ *Clear your mind:* Breathe slowly and deeply, right down to your stomach. Listen to the sound of your breath.

- *Approach the gateway:* Imagine you are walking through a wood. You reach a clearing. In the centre is a large stone with a sword embedded in it.

- *Take the test:* Grasp the handle of the sword and pull it firmly from the stone. If it doesn't work, try again another time. When you succeed, hold the sword up in triumph. You have passed the test.

- *The stairs:* Merlin steps forward and leads you to his tower. You go up a long winding stairway to his study at the top. The views are breathtaking.

- *Observe and explore:* Merlin unveils a large crystal sphere and bids you look within it. It's filled with swirling mist. As you gaze into it, you start to see forms. The shapes become clearer, and you can see people and scenes from your past lives in the world of magicians. Observe for as long as you wish.

- *Return:* When you feel ready to go, thank Merlin and let yourself return gently and smoothly to your everyday world.

CONCLUSION

A revolution in consciousness is underway. People are waking up to the hidden powers of the mind. New horizons are expanding in all directions. As we discover the magic of our past lives, a positive future becomes possible as well.

These new parameters of reality are also transforming the way we see ourselves in the present. As a result, key developments have been taking place in the field of psychology and counselling.

For some years now, influential people like Abraham Maslow, Stanislav Grof, Erich Fromm, Carl Rogers and Roberto Assagioli have been remapping the aims and purposes of psychotherapy. They have voiced what many in that world have been feeling for a long time: the traditional method of focusing only on mental problems gives a false view of patients and is not entirely helpful. Believing that happiness comes from meaningful, fulfilling lives, they have been aiming to develop a new kind of psychology – one that would be more holistic, including the heart and spirit as well as the mind. It would go beyond 'normality' as the benchmark ideal and actively nurture happiness, talent, wellness and growth. In 1998 Martin Seligman launched Positive Psychology based on these principles.

Transpersonal psychology and counselling take this a step further, focusing primarily on the spiritual side of consciousness. *The Journal of Transpersonal Psychology* describes it as being 'concerned with the study of humanity's highest potential'. Like Positive Psychology, the foundation belief of transpersonal psychology is that however well-adjusted the ego self may be, it is not the true source of happiness and fulfilment. That can only be found through spiritual self-development and awareness of our greater consciousness beyond the socialized identity.

Transpersonal psychology recontextualizes experience in positive and meaningful ways. For example, the ego self may see difficult events as signs of being a helpless victim of life. At the level of higher consciousness, however, we may realize that we deliberately chose those experiences to gain strength or learn something valuable.

As Ram Dass said, 'When you identify with your soul, you live in a loving universe.'

Discovering our former selves is part of this identity revolution. Past-life awareness may be one of the easiest and most direct ways to go beyond the ego self and all its associated difficulties. Pervasive issues such as gender and racial discrimination, co-dependency, victim consciousness and petty judgementalism all come from the illusion that the little self is all we are.

Carl Jung said that we don't solve our problems, we grow out of them. We never did fit into that cramped cage of the little ego self. As we rise above it, the distress it created will melt away like fog in the morning sun.

Past-life therapy began with following the traditional model of psychology by focusing on trauma-based issues. In some ways, it was simply an extension of looking for the source of problems in the patient's childhood. This approach has its validity and can be profoundly effective. However, like Positive Psychology, past-life awareness can bring us so much more than that. It automatically moves us beyond identifying too much with the current self and shows how meaningful and enriching an expanded consciousness can be.

As more people adopt this view, little by little it will change the world. Societies and institutions are based on the psychology and beliefs of the majority. When most people realize that they're spiritual beings who've had many lives, the petty tyranny of the ego will lose its power. When enough people stop suppressing their inner powers, outer oppressions will crumble away. A more benign way of life will then become possible. This is the highest form of magical power – transforming our consciousness and thus the world we live in.

I hope the personal accounts in this book have served to entertain you and perhaps reminded you of your own positive past memories and magical future potential. I also hope that many of you will find ways to take up the baton of new consciousness and forge ahead with exciting new discoveries.

May all the paths you take be joyful, rewarding and abundant at every level of your multi-dimensional self.

FURTHER READING

Roberto Assagioli, Maria Luisa Girelli and Sergio Bartoli, *Transpersonal Development: the Dimension Beyond Psychosynthesis*, Inner Way Productions/Smiling Wisdom, 2008

P. M. H. Atwater, *The Big Book of Near Death Experiences: The Complete Sourcebook*, Hampton Roads Publishing, 2007

Michael Baigent and Richard Leigh, *The Elixir and the Stone*, Arrow, 2005

Robert Bauval, *The Egypt Code*, Arrow, 2007

Frederick Bligh Bond, *The Gate of Remembrance*, Forgotten Books, 2012

Carol Bowman, *Children's Past Lives*, Thorsons, 1998

Eileen Caddy, *Flight into Freedom and Beyond*, Findhorn Press, 2002

Edgar Evans Cayce, *Edgar Cayce on Atlantis*, Little, Brown & Company, 2000

The Findhorn Community, *The Findhorn Garden Story*, Findhorn Press, 2008

Joe Fisher, *The Case for Reincarnation*, Somerville House Books, 1998

Dion Fortune, *Psychic Self-Defence: A Study in Occult Pathology and Criminality*, Red Wheel/Weiser, 1930

Dion Fortune and Gareth Knight, *The Magical Battle of Britain*, SIL Trading Ltd, 1993

Gerald B. Gardner, *Witchcraft Today*, Rider & Company, 1954

Stanislav Grof, MD, *Healing Our Deepest Wounds: The Holotropic Paradigm Shift*, Stream of Experience Productions, 2012

Michael Harner, *The Way of the Shaman*, HarperSanFrancisco, 1992

Jeffrey Iverson, *More Lives Than One?*, Macmillan, 1977

Gareth Knight, *Dion Fortune and The Inner Light*, Thoth Publications, 2000

Elisabeth Kübler-Ross and Raymond A. Moody, *Life After Life*, Rider, 2001

Robert Lomas, *Turning the Hiram Key*, Lewis Masonic, 2005

Joseph McMoneagle, *Remote Viewing Secrets: A Handbook*, Hampton Roads Publishing, 2000

Joseph McMoneagle, *Memoirs of a Psychic Spy: The Remarkable Life of U.S. Government Remote Viewer 001*, Hampton Roads Publishing, 2006

Lynne McTaggart, *The Field*, Element, 2003

Lynne McTaggart, *The Intention Experiment*, HarperElement, 2008

Abraham H. Maslow, *Toward a Psychology of Being*, Wilder Publications, 2011

Arnold Mindel, *Dreambody*, Deep Democracy Exchange, 2011

Jeff Merrifield, *Damanhur: The Story of the Extraordinary Italian Artistic and Spiritual Community*, Thorsons, 1998

Robert Monroe, *Journeys Out of the Body*, Souvenir Press, 1989

David Morehouse, *Psychic Warrior: True Story of the CIA's Paranormal Espionage Programme*, Clairview Books, 2000

Michael Newton, *Journey of Souls*, Llewellyn, 1994

Sheila Ostrander, *Psychic Discoveries Behind the Iron Curtain*, Souvenir Press, 1999

Lynn Picknett and Clive Prince, *The Templar Revelation*, Corgi, 2007

Carl Rogers, *On Becoming a Person*, Constable, 2004

Rupert Sheldrake, *The Rebirth of Nature*, Rider & Co., 1993

Ian Stevenson, *Twenty Cases Suggestive of Reincarnation*, University of Virginia Press, 1988

Michael Talbot, *The Holographic Universe*, HarperCollins, 1996

Russell Targ, *Limitless Mind: A Guide to Remote Viewing*, New World Library, 2004

Robert Tindall, *The Jaguar That Roams the Mind*, Park Street Press, 2008

Peter Tompkins and Christopher Bird, *The Secret Life of Plants*, HarperPerennial, 1989

Linda Tucker, *Mystery of the White Lions*, Hay House, 2010

Helen Wambach, *Reliving Past Lives*, Barnes & Noble, 1984

Lyall Watson, *Supernature*, Coronet Books, 1974

Colin Wilson, *The Occult*, Grafton Books, 1979

Benjamin Woolley, *The Queen's Conjurer: The Science and Magic of Dr. Dee*, Flamingo, 2002

Paramahansa Yogananda, *Autobiography of a Yogi*, Self-Realization Fellowship, 2006

JOIN THE HAY HOUSE FAMILY

As the leading self-help, mind, body and spirit publisher in the UK, we'd like to welcome you to our family so that you can enjoy all the benefits our website has to offer.

 EXTRACTS from a selection of your favourite author titles

 COMPETITIONS, PRIZES & SPECIAL OFFERS Win extracts, money off, downloads and so much more

 LISTEN to a range of radio interviews and our latest audio publications

 CELEBRATE YOUR BIRTHDAY An inspiring gift will be sent your way

 LATEST NEWS Keep up with the latest news from and about our authors

 ATTEND OUR AUTHOR EVENTS Be the first to hear about our author events

 **iPHONE APPS** Download your favourite app for your iPhone

 **HAY HOUSE INFORMATION** Ask us anything, all enquiries answered

join us online at **www.hayhouse.co.uk**

  Astley House, 33 Notting Hill Gate, London W11 3JQ
T: 020 3675 2450 E: info@hayhouse.co.uk

ABOUT THE AUTHOR

After graduating with a BA (Hons) degree, **Atasha Fyfe** taught high school History and English before entering the world of journalism. She knew in her heart, however, that these experiences were in many ways a preparation for her true calling.

Her deepest interest was spiritually-centred psychology, and to develop this she studied widely and took courses in Rogerian Counselling, Hypnotherapy and Transpersonal Psychology. She then felt inspired to move from London to Glastonbury, where she discovered that her clients were primarily interested in finding out about their past lives.

Realizing this was life's special gift to her, Atasha embraced the subject wholeheartedly. An experienced shaman gave her private tuition in past life regression, and she researched everything she could on the subject. At the same time, she began to regularly publish articles in New Age and esoteric magazines.

A fascinating journey unfolded, during which she built up a large data bank of case studies and made many exciting discoveries about the greater awareness and potentials that are available to us all.

If you'd like to share your own past life experiences and insights, you're welcome to contact Atasha through her website.

www.pastlivesglastonbury.co.uk